EDWARDIAN STORIES OF DIVORCE

To Sid and Ollie, who saw this book when it was only Notes in a heavy bookbag!

Here's to memories of London. love Tanci 2/24/94

EDWARDIAN STORIES OF DIVORCE

Janice Hubbard Harris

RUTGERS UNIVERSITY PRESS
New Brunswick, New Jersey

Library of Congress Cataloging-in-Publication Data

Harris, Janice Hubbard, 1943–
    Edwardian stories of divorce / Janice Hubbard Harris.
        p.   cm.
    Includes bibliographical references and index.
    ISBN 0-8135-2246-3 (cloth : alk. paper). — ISBN
    0-8135-2247-1 (pbk. : alk. paper)
        1. English prose literature—20th century—History and criticism.
    2. Divorce in literature.   3. Divorce—Law and legislation—Great
    Britain—History—20th century.   4. Literature and society—England—
    History—20th century.   5. Politics and literature—England—
    History—20th century.   6. Women and literature—England—
    History—20th century.   7. Domestic relations—England—
    History—20th century.   8. Marriage in literature.   I. Title.
    PR808.D58H37   1996
    828'.80809355—dc20   95-4572
                                                                 CIP
            British Cataloging-in-Publication information available

Frontis: "A Well-Balanced Household" by Dudley Tennant
(*The Windsor Magazine* 33, January 1911: 329).

To
Duncan Harris

CONTENTS

CONTENTS

LIST OF ILLUSTRATIONS

A C K N O W L E D G M E N T S

Writing *Edwardian Stories of Divorce* required time, access to the work of others, encouragement, and guidance. To those who provided, I am sincerely grateful.

For time, I thank the National Endowment for the Humanities who granted me a Senior Research Fellowship; the Trustees of the University of Wyoming and the Ed Flittie Sabbatical Award Committee who supported me with a sabbatical leave and months in London; Dean Oliver Walter of the College of Arts and Sciences and Mark Booth and Janet Constantinides of the Department of English who fostered a complementarity between the time I devoted to teaching and writing.

For access to the work of others, I thank the many efficient and friendly librarians I have relied on throughout the project, from the University of Wyoming's Interlibrary Loan staff, to librarians at the University of Colorado in Boulder, the British Library in London and Colindale, as well as the Fawcett Library and Law Library at Middle Temple in London.

For help in funding the book's illustrations and permissions, I thank Bill Gern, vice president of the University of Wyoming's Office of Research; for help in securing two of the illustrations, I thank Katherine Jensen and Audie Blevins. My appreciation goes also to Faber and Faber Ltd. for permission to quote from Philip Larkin's poem, "MCMXIV."

And lastly, for encouragement and guidance, I thank Leslie Mitchner, Tania Modleski, Susan McKay, Rosemary Daniell, Glenda Conway, Ann Ardis, my colleagues within the English Department and Women's

ACKNOWLEDGMENTS

Studies Program at the University of Wyoming, and my family. Leslie Mitchner's faith and criticism were crucial to the book, from inception to realization. Tania Modleski, Susan McKay, Rosemary Daniell, and Glenda Conway each gave encouraging words at distinct moments in the book's progress. Ann Ardis read a late draft, saw virtue in the enterprise, and made specific, helpful suggestions. My colleagues in English and Women's Studies were there when I needed them. Closing words of gratitude go to my family. In this book on divorce, I write of ties. Duncan, Adam, and Joshua Harris have provided me with the ties that bind human hearts and minds in the best sense.

EDWARDIAN STORIES OF DIVORCE

Such Innocence

Never such innocence,
Never before or since,
As changed itself to past
Without a word—the men
Leaving the gardens tidy,
The thousands of marriages
Lasting a little while longer:
Never such innocence again.
—Philip Larkin,
from "MCMXIV" (1964)

Useless for Hilda to take that casual tone! Useless for Edwin to hum! The unconcealable thought in each of their minds was—and each could divine the other's thought and almost hear its vibration:
"We might end in the divorce court, too."
Hence their self-consciousness.
The thought was absurd, irrational, indefensible, shocking. It had no father and no mother, it sprang out of naught; but it existed, and it had force enough to make them uncomfortable.
—Arnold Bennett, *These Twain* (1915)

This book has two purposes: to expand understanding of the Edwardian era and to complicate the stories we tell of divorce. In his pathbreaking study, *The Edwardian Turn of Mind,* Samuel Hynes cut through the nostalgia that blurred many earlier studies of the decade. Analyzing a series of tense internal divisions troubling Edwardians—rich versus poor, employer versus employee, English versus Irish, conservative versus liberal, and woman versus man—he gives brief but insightful attention to the debate over divorce.[1] After all, in an age anxious about rifts and ruptures, what rupture hits closer to home than divorce? But succeeding Edwardian scholars have generally lost sight of this debate, even scholars who have similarly emphasized internal divisions and/ or taken the family as their focus.[2] Today England experiences the highest rate of divorce within the European community.[3] Whether the focus is on Royals or plebeians, book after book and editorial after editorial ask where the country is heading on this issue.[4] *Edwardian Stories of Divorce* seeks to discover where the English stood on this issue when the twentieth-century conversation was launched.

Carrying what Lawrence Stone in *Road to Divorce* calls "a heavy baggage of passionately felt moral principles and symbolic meaning" (6) and raising a host of religious, economic, and social issues, the Edwardian debate over divorce was considered by many to be a holy war.[5] The sense of urgency rings clear in the words of Father Henry Day, S.J.: "If I were to be asked what institution it is that most of all injures society; or from what source flow the worst evils and miseries with which modern society is afflicted; what is the evil which most of all degrades public morality, I should have to answer, Divorce."[6] Advocates in the opposite camp speak with equal intensity. Sir Arthur Conan Doyle, who served for ten years as president of the Divorce Law Reform Union, sends out this call: "If a young man were entering life with money, brains, and an unselfish soul, and if he surveyed the whole field of human suffering and human endeavor to see where he might best throw all that he had into one good cause and so justify

his existence on earth, I do not think that he would find
one more suitable for his purpose than the reform of the
English divorce laws."[7] Divorce causes—or elimi-
nates—untold suffering. Liberalize divorce and destroy—or clean up—the nation. In ways recognizable
from America's debates over abortion and welfare reform, Edwardians on any side of any issue within the
divorce debate could quickly envision the future of the
nation riding on the outcome of the controversy.

An overreaction? Certainly. And yet, as Stone suggests, England's metamorphosis from a nonseparating
and nondivorcing culture into one where separation and
divorce are everyday events may be, in fact, as profound
a revolution as any the English have experienced in the
past five hundred years, for good or ill (422). Let me say
a word more about the Edwardians' sense of urgency.

In *The Trial of Madame Caillaux,* Edward Berenson
writes of the contemporaneous debate over divorce in
belle époque France. Like their Edwardian counterparts,
French politicians chanted the following equations:
Troubled families make for a troubled nation. The institution of marriage is the foundation of all other state
institutions. As marriage goes, so goes France. Asked
precisely *how* this is true, how the institution of marriage determines a nation more than the institutions of
government or marketplace, the answer was often tauto-
logical: It is true because it is true. Good fathers are equal
to good leaders. Good wives and children are equal to
good citizens. Like current commentators on American
politics, Berenson observes that politicians have much
to gain from repeating their refrain regarding the primacy of family values: If fathers would only be more
responsible, mothers more nurturing, marriages more

stable, and children more disciplined, the nation's problems would be solved. The spotlight is on the character of the nation's citizenry and not on the difficult legislative challenges (child care, health care, pay equity) facing the politician.

Given the transparency of the political posturing, then and now, this ranting on the primacy of marriage and family is easy to dismiss. But Phyllis Rose, in *Parallel Lives,* forces us to revisit the question, looking at the cultural importance of marriage less from the politician's point of view and more from the perspective of our own experiences and memories of family life. In her view, the day-in day-out practice of marriage can, in fact, lay some legitimate claim to being one of the primary institutions in Western culture. Be it our own or the one we observed our parents daily negotiating, for many Western peoples marriage remains the most intimate, long-term, direct, and detailed engagement in the structuring of power relations that they will experience. Is this very small state a democracy, oligarchy, or tyranny? Rose convincingly traces the links between an individual's sense of *husband* and *wife* and his or her sense of *liberty* and *authority* in other human relations. Marriage urgently matters. So therefore does divorce.

The English debate over divorce did not begin with the Edwardians. Stone chooses 1530 as the year from which to launch his study of the English road to divorce. In *The Development of the Family and Marriage in Europe,* Jack Goody begins with pre-Christian practices. Roderick Phillips, in *Putting Asunder,* starts with Roman Catholic doctrine from the Middle Ages. Mary Ann Glendon suggests that, in fact, there is no historically accurate starting point on this issue, not in England nor elsewhere. In *Abortion and Divorce in Western Law,* she advises us to see divorce as a universal and perennial social concern, neither solved nor solvable, rather more or less wisely understood and regulated from community to community, century to century (1–2, 75). As I hope to show, the Edwardian debate comprises a very lively set of exchanges regarding this ongoing topic of human conversation.

If expanding our understanding of the Edwardian era is one aim of the book, the second is to complicate the stories we tell about divorce. Writing about five Victorian marriages, Rose observes that easy stories drive out hard ones. Faced with the primal stew of data that makes up a marriage, we respond with an act of the imagination, a narrative. This response Rose sees as inevitable, part of what it is to be human. But all too often our narratives are shaped according to a simple rather than a complicated paradigm.

Rose's point respecting marriage and narrative holds true for much of the storytelling that accompanies divorce. As Catherine K. Reissman in the United States and Danny Danziger, Gwynn Davis, and Mervyn Murch in England demonstrate, women and men who have recently gone through a divorce show a powerful need to shape the experience into a coherent narrative.[8] It must have a beginning, middle, and end; there must be an allocation of blame and an explanation for the catastrophe with which one can live. To insist that the true story behind a failed marriage is irretrievable, a stance taken by recent English divorce law, disturbs, unsettles, frustrates.[9] Something happened. We want to know what— and we want others to know. But as Danziger's collection of divorce interviews makes painfully clear, indeed as our own experiences of listening and talking often indicate, the complex "something" can all too easily get reduced in the telling.

If personal narratives of marriage and divorce can be reductive, so too can historical narratives. Here, the teller reacts against the difficult times he or she lives in by envisioning a rosier past, a time of "such innocence." Barraged by current predictions in England and the United States that one in three marriages will end in divorce, one says nostalgically, things were not always thus. Gardens were tidy, marriages lasted, people were different. Once upon a time people lived according to a better story: It was death till you part, and so you made the best of it. People were happier in the long run.

Statistics back up aspects of this story. In England, the average annual number of divorces at the beginning of the century was between five and six hundred, out of a population of 6.6 million married couples (Stone 6, 435). That yields an annual rate of approximately .08 divorces per 1,000 married couples. Eighty years later, the number had risen to 160,000 divorces per year, with an annual rate of 13.4 divorces per 1,000 married couples (Stone 436). And the rates continue to rise. John Haskey's well-known prediction that 33 percent of English marriages will end in divorce has recently been revised upward to 37 percent.[10]

I do not dispute the profound effect that the rising number of divorces is having on individual English lives, social services, and the nation's sense of itself at the close of this century. There is a revolution going on. I do, however, dispute Philip Larkin's image of an Edwardian age of innocence. On this issue, Arnold Bennett, an Edwardian, is our better guide. Thoughts of divorce were pervasive and were making everyone uncomfortable. To assume that early in the century, divorce was not to be done and therefore not to be contemplated is simply inaccurate.[11]

Focusing on divorce in Edwardian England, this book complements sections of O. R. McGregor's classic *Divorce in England,* Phillips's *Putting Asunder,* Jacqueline Burgoyne's *Divorce Matters,* and Stone's *Road to Divorce.* In focusing more specifically on the way divorce was being represented during that era—on the stories that were being told in the heat of the debate—it allies itself more with work done by Reissman, Danziger, Thomas Deegan, John Eekelaar, Carol Smart, Glendon, and Berenson.[12]

Each of the latter, while coming at the issue of divorce from different angles, contends that the way in which people envision divorce—what it is, what causes it, and what we do about it—is as central to its reality as are tables of data and particular statutes. Data and laws tell stories, as Eekelaar, Smart, and Glendon emphasize; but, in turn, a culture's stories shape the data and the laws. Stories influence how data are gathered, structured, and interpreted. They have a powerful effect on how laws are written, enforced, respected, defied, or ignored.

What then was the Edwardian story on divorce? I begin by reviewing some of the cases, laws, procedures, and statistics that were pressuring Edwardians into storytelling on this difficult issue.

The Case of Mrs. Pineapple Dodd

On April 22, 1906, Sir John Gorell Barnes, president of England's Divorce Court, reluctantly denied a divorce to Mrs. Pineapple Dodd.[13] The facts of the case were these. Mr. and Mrs. Dodd had married in 1891 and had one child. Five years into the marriage, Mr. Dodd was drinking heavily, failing to provide for the family, and, indeed, living off Mrs. Dodd's earnings as a domestic. On August 21, 1896, he walked out. On September 9, Mrs. Dodd, in response, went to her local magistrate and got a separation order on the grounds of willful neglect. That order allowed her legally to live apart from Mr. Dodd and ordered him to contribute maintenance to her and the child. She and the child moved in with her mother and remained there for nine years, never receiving a farthing from Mr. Dodd. Then, in 1905, Mrs. Dodd gathered clear evidence of Mr. Dodd's infidelity. She petitioned for a divorce. Presenting her case in the Royal Courts of Justice on December 19, 1905, she cited Mr. Dodd's previous desertion and current adultery. Had she been successful, she could have remarried and started a new life.[14]

But she was not successful. Gorell Barnes explained why: Like thousands of similarly placed wives since the Separation Acts of the 1880s and 1890s, when Mrs. Dodd legally separated from her unsatisfactory husband, she effectively barred the way to an eventual divorce. To obtain that longed-for clean break, as everyone familiar with the law knew, she would need to prove his adultery plus an additional cause, most often desertion for two years or cruelty. Adultery that involved rape, sodomy, bestiality, or bigamy also constituted a ground.[15] In this case, Mr. Dodd's desertion technically had only been in effect from August 21 to September 9, a far cry from the required two years. In truth, the lay-about Dodd seemed eager to return and live off his commendable wife.

Nor could any of the other additional acts be alleged. For example, given the separation order, there had been no opportunity for cruelty. The *decree nisi* was denied.[16]

Given his negative decision, Gorell Barnes had no reason to address child custody in the Dodd case. But current readers may find background on this issue useful in gaining an understanding of Edwardian divorce practice. Would Mrs. Dodd have been granted custody of their child if the divorce had gone through? Undoubtedly. By 1906, a father's unquestioned right to the custody of all children born of the marriage had been undermined, owing largely to Caroline Norton's campaign in the late 1830s. Infant Custody Acts passed in 1839 and 1873, as well as the Divorce Act of 1857, gave the courts increasing discretion in deciding which parent should have custody and access, first of children up to age seven and then up to age sixteen. The Act of 1873 also removed the bar that had previously prohibited a mother found guilty of adultery from even petitioning the court. The Infant Custody Act of 1886, while it had more to do with issues related to the guardianship of children after the death of one parent, established the welfare of the child as the primary principle that should guide the courts.[17] In practice, wives who succeeded in divorcing husbands—something they could not have managed had they not been deemed spotless in the eyes of the court—tended to be given custody of the children. Presumably, this would have been the situation with Mrs. Dodd. Wives who had been found guilty of adultery rarely received custody.[18] The assumption was, no matter how good a mother she had been, her adultery so affected her relations with her children as to make her a bad influence.[19]

As suggested above, what Gorell Barnes saw in the
Dodd case was a complex set of legal cross purposes, a
confusion so troubling that he felt obliged to break with
normal practice and publish a comment on his ruling.
He asked the public to consider the fact that any separated husband desiring a divorce was essentially rewarded for committing adultery *and* desertion, cruelty,
rape, bigamy, bestiality, etc. For two wrongful acts
would get him his divorce, with the liberty to remarry
and often with a lesser responsibility for maintenance
than he may have had under his separation order. By
committing "only" adultery or cruelty or desertion, he
and his estranged wife were relegated to a lifelong
limbo, neither together nor asunder, wed nor free. Consider further, he urged, the inequity in the treatment
of women and men: Whereas wives were required to
prove adultery plus an additional cause, husbands
needed only to prove their wife's adultery.

And what about cost? For most of the Dodds of England, that is, for the 80 percent of the population that
was working class,[20] the very possibility of suing for a
divorce was financially impossible. The records do not
indicate how Mrs. Dodd financed her petition, but if she
did apply for legal aid by suing in *forma pauperis,* she
would have had to show that she was earning less than
thirty shillings a week and that all her worldly posses-
sions, from pots and pans to furniture and blankets,
were in sum worth less than twenty-five pounds (*Report
of the Royal Commission* 1:11). Tales told by witnesses to
the Royal Commission speak of years of saving, of
friends and family contributing to the risky venture.
The actual costs consisted of court and solicitor bills; the
expenses incurred by compensating one's witnesses

(doctors, clergy, hotel maids, etc.); travel and overnight accommodations if anyone important to the case lived outside of London; and the loss of wages through missing work. A. Musgrave, registrar for the Divorce Division of the High Courts of Justice, estimated a minimal cost of between forty and sixty pounds for an undefended suit, depending partly on whether the parties lived in or near London.[21] As did other witnesses to the Royal Commission, he emphasized that the cost and restrictive legal aid procedures were creating virtually insurmountable barriers for the vast majority of England's citizens. Musgrave's figures show approximately fifty cases per annum brought forward in *forma pauperis (Report of the Royal Commission* 1: 11, 16).

Problems with grounds, gender equity, and cost: All of these troubled Gorell Barnes. But there was another underlying concern, one related to legal jurisdiction. I say more below about the Separation Acts, but at the time of the Dodd case, English wives or husbands could go to their local police court and receive a separation order, allowing them legally to live apart, with the husband ordered to pay maintenance for wife and children. And English wives and husbands were doing so by the thousands. As Gorell Barnes saw it, too many people were getting separation orders for trivial complaints. The magistrates handing out the orders were in no way properly trained to handle these matters and demanded nothing like the proof required in a higher court.[22] The results were 1) a proliferation of separated men and women, put asunder through a lax process and having no chance at a second legal marriage; and 2) people like Mrs. Dodd coming to the divorce court after a separation order and presenting the judge of the Divorce

Court with legal confusions. Implied in Gorell Barnes's critique of the jurisdiction problem is his desire to broaden the grounds and facilities for divorce so as to redirect marital complaints away from the lower courts of summary jurisdiction toward higher, stricter courts. In brief, he would strengthen the institution of marriage by granting a few more divorces in order to prevent so many separations.

In what became an oft-quoted comment from the Dodd ruling, Gorell Barnes summed up the English divorce law as "full of inconsistencies, anomalies, and inequities, amounting almost to absurdities." He sent Mrs. Dodd on her way with the comment, "And it will not be any satisfaction to her to know that if her case had arisen . . . in . . . most other civilized countries, she would have succeeded."[23] (I must add that had Mrs. Dodd's case arisen under another English judge, she probably also would have succeeded. Precedent in her kind of case ignored technicalities and accepted the wife's claim that the husband had deserted.[24] In general, Edwardian wives fared well in the divorce court, winning decrees even more consistently than their husbands.[25]) As J.E.G. DeMontmorency explains, Gorell Barnes longed for a Royal Commission on Divorce, one that would go where no similar body had ever gone before. This commission would so thoroughly examine the complex religious, social, sexual, political, economic, and medical issues involved in divorce that its recommendations would establish a clear and beneficent twentieth-century policy for England that would serve as a model to the rest of Europe.[26]

Responding to the Call

In the view of E.S.P. Haynes, a prolific writer and organizer on divorce reform throughout the decade, Gorell Barnes's judgment in the Dodd case galvanized the reform movement. Inherently difficult and unattractive to legislators, the issue had been far from popular up to that point. Lord Russell had given it visibility with his unsuccessful bills of 1902 and 1903.[27] But in general, serious discussion of the problem had been hard to foster. In the press, writes Haynes, there was a "fierce taboo" against debating the issues.[28] Coverage was limited to the reporting of cases. Indeed, Haynes recalls attending a meeting of one of the struggling divorce reform societies in July 1905.[29] Five people attended; Haynes himself was ready to disband. Then came the "fearless utterances" of Gorell Barnes and the movement took off. "It soon became a snowball. The press were induced to take up the subject, and when once the taboo of silence was broken, they found it good copy."[30]

In the years following Gorell Barnes's judgment, books, articles, editorials, and novels poured forth, reaching a peak during and immediately following the hearings of the Royal Commission on Divorce and Matrimonial Causes of 1910–1912. George Bernard Shaw devotes his entire preface to *Getting Married* to a biting review of the issues raised by the hearings. As Christina Sinclair Bremner, writing in 1912, attests, "Few subjects of profound human interest have aroused more controversy and conflict than the question of divorce."[31]

Why did the movement rise to such prominence at just this time? As Stone writes, changes in English di-

vorce law were extremely rare and thought best avoided
by governments with other agendas (6). Gorell Barnes
was opening an issue that had been effectively closed
since 1857. (Nor, after 1912, would another commission on divorce be appointed until the 1950s.)

Edwardian Cecil Chapman listed a set of possible reasons. Whereas in previous times, Chapman wrote, the
home was necessarily a training ground and economic
unit, by the beginning of the twentieth century it was
more idealistically thought of as a refuge and resting
place. Married women could get work outside it; children, now at school, were no longer being trained under
its roof. In other ways as well, writes Chapman, Edwardian wives were developing a clearer sense of themselves as independent beings, conceiving for themselves
a different morality than that of self-sacrifice. Along the
same lines, husbands and wives in general were increasingly valuing themselves as individuals, created to pur-
sue happiness. Institutions should serve them rather
than they serve the institution. Who would stay in a bad
marriage in order to support "the Institution of Marriage"? Finally, expectations were rising regarding domestic happiness and companionable marriage.[32]

To read Chapman's explanations for the Edwardians'
increased interest in divorce is to nod in vague assent,
but also to find questions arising. Working-class Edwardians calling for reforms, especially in the cost of
obtaining a divorce, were far from experiencing their
homes as resting places that they could afford to leave
when the going got rough. As Chapman himself recog-
nizes elsewhere, the working-class home was still very
much an economic unit, one that financially suffered
terribly if husband or wife decamped.

Nor is the evidence at all clear that English wives of

any class during this era were increasingly independent and/or working for wages. It is true that the Married Women's Property Acts passed in 1870 and 1882 purported to give married women some independence by allowing them control over their "separate" property. But the 1870 law mainly addressed the *earnings* of a married woman and, even then, such earnings as she had accumulated after her marriage.[33] If few Edwardian wives were bringing in wages—an issue I address below—such a protection could mean little in the main. The Act of 1882 went further, giving a married woman control over property "of whatever kind and from whatever source" she possessed before or after her marriage.[34] But again, if the vast number of Edwardian wives owned no separate property, in earnings or other forms, these protections had little practical effect.[35]

Were Edwardian wives increasingly working for wages? Louise Tilly and Joan W. Scott argue that married women's waged work had actually declined since the middle of the nineteenth century.[36] Nancy Folbre demonstrates that the available data are so unreliable as to make any generalizations suspect.[37] If we seek documentation from feminist texts of the decade we still get little evidence of waged activity for wives. In fact, we encounter evidence to the contrary. The suffrage play "How the Vote Was Won" by Cicely Hamilton and Christopher St. John pits the presumably useless wife, Ethel, against husband Horace's brave, resourceful, and unmarried female relatives, all of whom are out working for wages. In the same vein, Hamilton's *Marriage as a Trade* and Olive Schreiner's *Woman and Labour* castigate Edwardian wives for their utter dependence on wage-earning mates. Schreiner makes much of what she sees as the parasitism of wives, even wives of the working class. Coming from another angle, the superb suffrage monologue, "Jim's Leg" by L. S. Phibbs, urges recognition of the housewife's many tasks, but the image remains of the Edwardian wife as generally unengaged in waged labor.[38]

As for changing psychological expectations respecting marriage and individual happiness, scholars today cite similar shifts in expectations as reasons for our own late twentieth-century liberalizations of divorce. This suggests that these attitudinal causes, if pertinent in a broad sense, are too general to be of much use in seeking the origin of any particular debate.[39]

To listen closely to the many stories of divorce being constructed by Edwardians is to speculate on a set of causes more specific to the decade: 1) England's sense of vulnerability vis-à-vis the rest of Europe, and Germany in particular; 2) its fear of a declining population and/or "racial" degeneration; 3) an anxiety over the increasing number of people separating; and 4) David Lloyd George's social agenda, with its challenge to the traditional lines of separation between public law and private life.[40]

In *The New Machiavelli*—which opens in the wake of the narrator's divorce—H. G. Wells writes of his protagonist's previous tendency to draw a mental map of the globe that left Europe more or less invisible while prominently featuring England and its empire. That mental map changed for the narrator in the early years of the twentieth century. Increasingly, he felt that his European neighbors were "going ahead of us, mentally alert while we fumbled, disciplined while we slouched . . . I began to have a distinct sense . . . of busy searchlights over the horizon" (132–133). What was going on in Europe began to seem highly relevant to Edwardians, and, seeking out allies in the opposite direction, so did what was going on in America. In this context, England perceived itself to be a real anomaly on the issue of divorce and all it implied about the right way to foster domestic orderliness and strength.[41] The perception was accurate, but this anomalousness was, in fact, of long standing.

Up until 1857, England had been distinguishing itself from all of its Protestant European neighbors and from America by being the only country to retain the Catholic prohibition against all divorce (Stone 7). As indicated above, when England opened the door to divorce, it did so grudgingly, setting up effective obstacles respecting cost and grounds.[42] The English rate of divorce from 1857 to 1914 was, in Stone's words, "statistically minute" (387). Across the Channel, things were different. In France, the courts would automatically grant a divorce upon proof of adultery and/or upon either partner being sentenced to severe criminal punishment. Cruelty or insult constituted grounds upon which the court could use its discretion. These grounds applied to husbands and wives alike. Local courts handled the cases, and financial assistance was available.[43] To England's 494 divorce decrees granted in 1900, France had 8,220. To England's 577 in 1913, France had 16,335 (Savage 511). In Germany, again a hovering presence in England's consciousness, the absolute grounds included infidelity, bigamy, desertion, and unnatural intercourse. Grounds upon which the court could use its discretion included dishonorable and immoral conduct, serious neglect of marital duties, and serious maltreatment (Phillips 431). The average annual number of decrees in

Germany between 1910 and 1913 was 13,008 (Phillips 517). In America the picture was complicated by the fact that divorce laws were determined by individual states. As Edwardians discussed America on this issue, South Carolina was famous for allowing no divorce, South Dakota infamous for allowing it on a wide range of grounds—impotence, fraud, adultery, cruelty, desertion, neglect, habitual intemperance, conviction for felony—and for requiring a mere ninety days' residence to establish state citizenship. The number of divorces in America in 1910 was a whopping 83,045 (Phillips 463).

In comparing themselves to continental Europe and America, English citizens, of course, disagreed on the significance of their anomalous stance. For reformers like Wells, England's domestic policies seemed a dangerous muddle. For conservatives, England's peculiarity stood as a light in the night of modern waywardness. But the point remains: As England was increasingly forced to scrutinize its domestic policies with an eye to how the nation stacked up against potential enemies and allies, its singular stance on divorce became more obvious and commanded social attention. Significantly, the very first order of business for the Royal Commission was a comparison of England and other countries.

"Falling Birth-Rate: Registrar-General's Alarming Figures": as the headlines of the *Evening Standard and St. James Gazette* for January 30, 1909, announced, the Seventieth Annual Report of the Registrar-General of Births, Deaths, and Marriages in England and Wales for the year 1907 showed England's birthrate at its lowest point on record, that is, 26.3 per 1,000 of total population. Conservatives claimed that liberalizing divorce would lead to a further drop. Advocates for reform argued that divorce, by allowing for remarriage, would not only encourage a rise in the birthrate but also address the problem of illegitimacy.[44]

Fear of a shrinking population certainly played into the divorce debate, but equally important were fears of a physically and mentally degenerating population. As Carol Dyhouse points out, in recruiting for the Boer War, England had been shocked by its high rates of infant mortality and the poor physical condition of many potential recruits.[45] Poverty and "social inefficiency" were affecting the constitutions of England's young people, undermining their ability to learn, earn, defend the realm, and bear children. From a different direction, the nascent science of eugenics was raising the specter of mental deterioration. If careful breeding could improve the race, careless breeding could do the opposite, increasing the number of the insane and mentally deficient. How could changes in the divorce laws affect this? As Phillips writes, many early eugenicists believed that certain conditions in the environment (bad homes) led to certain human tendencies (immorality or a lack of "civic worth"). In a matter of one or two generations, these tendencies became biologically inheritable (507, 510). People opposed to divorce contended that expanding the facilities for divorce would vastly increase the number of broken homes. These "pandemoniums of domestic misery" and "infernos of social corruption" would breed feeble-minded, amoral, social degenerates (Day 38). To the contrary, argued the voices for liberalization: Allow divorce and you will rescue women and men chained to alcoholic or insane partners and forced to bear their potentially defective children. In Bremner's view, England's strict divorce polices were inducing "debility and enervation, where the race should be strong and vigorous."[46]

To turn from the Edwardians' nervousness respecting enemies, allies, and their own population to their concerns over the increase in separation orders invites a further look at anxieties respecting domestic rifts and ruptures. As family law had developed over the preceding two decades, more women and eventually men of all classes were receiving the state's permission to separate. Between 1878 and 1902, the legal grounds for separating steadily broadened to include adultery, desertion, persistent cruelty, neglect or failure to maintain, and habitual drunkenness. When Gorell Barnes called for divorce law reform, the number of separation orders being granted by magistrates was averaging around 7,000 a year.[47] Nor, many people asserted, did those numbers begin to tell the whole story. Witnesses to the Royal Commission testified to an increasing number of informally separated couples who bypassed the local courts and went on with their lives practicing the extralegal "poor man's law."

To allow people to separate is to respond to the often brutal conditions of a marriage gone wrong, but what happens after the couple has separated? The subsequent problems cried out for further reform, in particular, the immense difficulty in getting separated husbands to support their children and the tendency for separated husbands and wives to take up with new partners and bear illegitimate children. As Gorell Barnes argued, separated people should be able to remarry. And that meant that separated people must be able to get a divorce.

Clearly seen as troublesome here are citizens living outside the ties that bind people to moral and religious

traditions—and also bind them financially to each other
and not to the state. Writing of early nineteenth-century
fears of trade unions or labor combinations, Nancy
Armstrong analyzes the way in which those fears shaped
the establishment's image of working-class corruption.
To describe how the poor are corrupt, conservatives
emphasized the dangerous "combinations" in which the
poor lived and bred, for example, their stewing, crawl-
ing rooms, their crowded alleyways and pubs. All was
close, stuffy, festering, divisionless—in brief, danger-
ously *combined*.[48] In looking at Edwardian fears of internal divisions, one sees the establishment constructing a
very different image of corruption. It is the unattached
person, wandering outside the closed room, who is cor-
rupted and corrupting. Especially horrifying was the
image of the woman with no ties to a private domicile.
Saying she was "on the streets" said it all. In the view of
Thomas Holmes, a frequent and generally sympathetic
commentator on issues related to the poor, she was almost inevitably a drunk or prostitute, loathsome, gross,
and dirty. All too often, he argued, she was ending her
days supported by the state.[49]

In short, whether one was pro-reform or anti-reform,
the tendency was to see separated people as a problem.
One could argue for divorce as a step toward remarriage
or against divorce as a way of keeping people tied to
their original contract: In either case, one is not seeing
the separated person as positively independent and productive. The lone male or female seems unrestrained,
irresponsible, drifting, dangerous, destitute, the sad
product of a rift.

This fear that what ought to be "inside" is "outside"
leads to the fourth Edwardian issue fueling the debate

on divorce, that is, a changing conceptualization of the relationship between public and private spheres initiated by David Lloyd George's social welfare program.

To say that any individual's survival and well-being is absolutely the private concern of him- or herself and family is to follow an understanding written down in the Renaissance. As Eekelaar and Mavis Maclean summarize that Renaissance pact, "It was the obligation of 'the father and grandfather and the mother and grandmother, and the children, of every poor, lame, and impotent person,' if they had the means, to 'relieve and maintain' such a person."[50] The state functions solely to enforce this assumption of private responsibility. Only in extreme cases, when a person cannot survive on his or her own and has no family, does the state reluctantly step in through a poor law scheme. But Lloyd George's social agenda was fundamentally challenging this old demarcation between private and public responsibility. Following the model provided by an apparently thriving Germany, Lloyd George argued that a wise state will positively and actively invest in the people's well being.[51] Through taxes, it will build decent housing and support people in their infancy, youth, and old age, in pregnancy, illness, alcoholism, and during times of unemployment.

This opening the door of formerly private family space to state presence worked not only to let the state in, but also to let the family out. How the daily, "natural" ways of family life were socially constructed became an important subject for investigation. Among other groups, Edwardian feminists offered especially cogent analyses of the ways in which the practice of marriage is constructed by specific social policies. Cicely Hamilton, Olive Schreiner, Clementina Black, and Maud Pember Reeves all offer tough critiques, for example, of the concept of the "family wage." Industry assumed that the wage earned by a man—any man, wed or single, responsible or otherwise—was really a "family wage," devoted to maintaining a cluster of people. The wage of a woman—any woman—was not so devoted, never mind the Mrs. Dodds of the world. That assumption, feminists argued, shaped many of the most intimate aspects of Edwardian courtship and marriage. It made women and children economically dependent and vulnerable; it made marriage, in Hamilton's words, a "trade" or industry like any other, though one singularly disadvantageous for the employee.

The point is this: As the state went in to nurture the family through a range of social programs, the family came out to be scrutinized by feminists and others as a social construction. And the moment "marriage" and "the family" are seen as something other than unchanging and natural practices—the moment reformers interested in school lunches or old age pensions or prenatal care march into the presumed privacy of family space— one of the taboos against discussing divorce is undermined. Marital failure becomes one more private concern open to public scrutiny. It was not that significant numbers of Edwardians actually rushed to the law. Again, divorce rates remained stable throughout the Edwardian decade. It is the possibility of English divorce that goes public.

Doing Justice to the Stories

In this book, I construct a story about other people's stories. What line does my own narrative take? I began this project with a broad interest in Edwardian representations of marriage.[52] Carol Smart's trenchant comment that nothing makes the contract of marriage more visible than a divorce and my fascination with the *Report of the Royal Commission on Divorce and Matrimonial Causes* inspired a specific interest in the Edwardian debate over divorce.[53] Smart made me realize that any genuine understanding of Edwardian representations of marriage cannot ignore this debate. The *Report,* three volumes of verbatim testimony and a fourth volume of recommendations and appendices, conveys with extraordinary power the voices of the time— articulate, troubled, and above all disparate. As I began to examine other Edwardian texts featuring narratives of divorce, the impression of cacophony only increased. How to analyze the range of representations in a way that respected the complexity of this national conversation?

My initial attempts organized the narratives by gender. The predictable story here would portray Edwardian women rising up en masse and demanding greater access to divorce while Edwardian men looked on in horror. But that story is much too easy. The exciting and verifiable finding is that English women were publicly speaking out and being heard for the first time in a social debate on divorce. They came as witnesses to the Royal Commission; they served on the commission itself; they wrote pamphlets, book-length analyses, and novel after novel. But they did not agree with each other. Nor should that surprise us.

As current studies of divorce indicate, there is not now and never has been a coherent woman's story on divorce. No more is there a unified man's story. There is not even a coherent feminist story on the issue. As Smart writes, late twentieth-century feminists concerned with divorce can disagree with each other from the very outset of the discussion. One group argues that it is futile to expend energies on legal reform because the law itself is a patriarchal practice. The other counters that such a dismissal oversimplifies the nature of the law and the dynamics of power relations.[54] Those feminists who do advocate legal reform differ in turn on which reforms truly benefit women. For example, do women gain or lose when divorce negotiations move out of the courts and into mediation procedures?[55] Did the move to no-fault grounds help or hurt women?[56] Is the practice of awarding child custody to the mother necessarily a victory?[57]

Victorian and Edwardian feminists were similarly at odds. For example, a fundamental decision for the Edwardian feminist committed to the suffrage campaign was whether or not to join the divorce law reform movement at all, knowing that such an allegiance would deflect energies from the campaign for the vote.[58] Those feminists who were willing to speak out on divorce split on a range of issues: the economic challenges that would face divorced women; grounds; the wisdom of mediation practices; alimony.[59] In *Feminism and the Family in England 1880–1939*, Dyhouse pushes our awareness of feminist disagreement over divorce a step further by pointing out the deep ambivalence experienced by individual feminists within their own hearts and minds. For some Victorian and Edwardian feminists, marriage was to be avoided, period. But for many more, family life provided "both their greatest source of emotional satisfaction, and yet also the root of their deepest frustrations" (185).

In brief, organizing the Edwardian narratives on divorce according to the gender of the storyteller raised more problems than it solved. Could the narratives somehow be organized by the economic class of the subjects under discussion or of the speakers? As one would expect, class enters the conversation at every turn. For example, everyone understood that the cost of divorce was keeping working-class people from seeking relief. But whether that harmed or benefited working-class husbands and wives was up for debate, by voices within the working class and elsewhere. Arguments about broadening grounds, restricting the publicizing of trials, and/or eradicating the distinction between male and female adultery simply multiplied the areas of disagreement. Again, the news here is that working-class voices were solicited and heard, most dramatically through a pair of surveys of working-class women conducted under the respective auspices of the Mothers' Union and the Women's Cooperative Guild. (See Appendix II.) But to orchestrate Edwardian voices or stories according to class implies false unities and ignores intraclass debates.

A more useful approach to the range of narratives has been one that looks less to some essential experience of marital failure shared by women or men, the middle class or the working class—an experience that then determines the narratives each group tells—and more to the narrative situations that elicited the Edwardians' stories of divorce. As many narrative theorists have observed, storytelling never occurs in a vacuum. Crucial to the content of any story are the circumstances under which it is told. What is the teller seeking? What can the listener give or withhold? What social and/or literary conventions, stated or unstated, shape the telling and listening? To ask these questions is to recognize that any large, contentious, national conversation will take place in different arenas, and these arenas will powerfully influence what stories get told. In this kind of analysis, the gender and class of the speakers and listeners will be foregrounded or muted according to the storytelling dynamics operating in a particular arena.

In deciding to organize this book according to the Edwardian arenas most productive of narratives on divorce, I have focused on the tabloid press, the Hearings of the Royal Commission on Divorce and Matrimonial Causes, and the novel. As I analyze the tales produced in these arenas, I make use of the concepts of stock story and counterstory, as these terms have recently been used by theorists of legal narrative.

The stock story, as Gerald Lopez describes it in "Lay Lawyering," is the conventional take on any controversial issue, from settling a taxi cab dispute to adjudicating a formal trial. Stock stories reinforce the culture's overarching reigning narratives on, say, individual rights, civilized behavior, constraints and mobilities. In the Edwardian debate over divorce, for example, the stock story promulgates the understanding that wives who stray from marital homes are shameful and dangerous. To Lopez's description of the stock story, Richard Delgado adds the complementary phenomenon of the counterstory.[60] Produced by outsiders, the counterstory does not simply refute the stock story on its own terms.

It brings new information, a different perspective, an unsettling angle. In a dispute over individual rights, a counterstory may introduce a discussion of mutual responsibilities. In a debate over wifely mobility, a counterstory may reconfigure the image of the house. Not surprisingly, some social arenas encourage stock stories, some counterstories.

In the Edwardian context, the key producers of stock stories on divorce were the courtroom and press. Chapter 1 looks at the tabloid coverage of the divorce trial, tracing the Edwardians' reigning tale on failed marriages, how they might and might not be dissolved, and what the consequences of seeking a divorce would be. In Chapter 2, the focus shifts to the flood of counterstories inspired by the hearings of the Royal Commission on Divorce and Matrimonial Causes. What was wrong with the stock stories circulated by the tabloids? Just about everything, according to many of the witnesses who testified. The hearings were designed to listen to arguments for and against reform, and indeed the commissioners ended up with a split vote on a central issue—the extending of grounds. But the dynamics operating in the hearings were such as to encourage local narratives aimed at change while discouraging narratives reinforcing the status quo. As I examine how stories of divorce were constructed in this arena, I look carefully at the way women participated and the way witnesses addressed the concerns of the working class. Chapter 3 turns to the novel, arguing that the divorce novel not only introduces topics unexplored in the other arenas but also intriguingly modifies the standoff one sees between the counterstories produced by the Royal Commission and the stock stories produced by trial and tabloid. Partly because of the conventions that rule the genre, the novels are able to explore genuine ambivalence. In the very presentation of its argument, a novel can sympathetically entertain the opposition. The debate *between* the other arenas is often reconfigured here as an inner dialogue within a character's mind. Self speaks to soul, duty to desire.

As indicated above, my aim is to complicate the stories we tell about divorce and about the Edwardian era. Looking at England's current practices, John Eekelaar writes that the old story on marriage and divorce was torn up with the Divorce Reform Act of 1969 and no new story has arisen to take its place.[61] Thus England's frequent altering of its divorce laws. Thus its sense of floundering on the issue. I contend that sixty years earlier, people all over England were dreaming of just such a tearing up. The dreams are long since gone, but the stories they inspired are very much to hand.

Stock Stories: Read All About It

When Mrs. Dodd went to trial with her petition for a divorce, she had to turn her back on the bustling noise of the Strand, pass through the iron gates of the Royal Courts of Justice, walk through the imposing Great Hall, enter an oak-paneled courtroom and tell her story to Sir Gorell Barnes, who would have been sitting in powdered wig and flowing robe as one of the courts' three presiding Lord Justices. Also in attendance would have been a bevy of similarly attired barristers, sundry clerks and solicitors, the press, and whatever members of the public had dropped in on the divorce court that particular day. Although the depiction of a divorce trial in the *Illustrated London News* on June 11, 1910, indicates a jury, most cases were tried by a judge.[1] (See Illustration 1.)

The semiotic system of the building delivers a clear message. Looking down on you as you progress toward the courts are the eyes of the wise. High up against the sky, above the suggestion of a rose window, stands a large statue of Jesus. Flanking him, a bit lower down, are King Solomon and King Alfred. Moving through the iron gates, one passes beneath the porches, elaborately carved with busts of England's eminent judges and lawyers. Enter into the great hall and the system becomes even more insistent. The eighty-foot-high ceilings, the stained glass windows, the richly patterned mosaic floor in tones of black, white, cream, sienna, and gold—all convey the atmosphere of a cathedral. The

OPPOSITE: *1 An Edwardian Divorce Trial*
(Illustrated London News, *June 11, 1910: 919*).

judgments rendered here are those of the Almighty, who presides over English justice. Had you been Mrs. Dodd, you might have wished there was at least one wise female looking down at you, perhaps even cheering you on. Queen Victoria is there, in a painting on the east wall, but she is clearly preoccupied with the December 4, 1882, ceremonies that opened these impressive buildings.[2]

The actual trials take place in a series of formal courtrooms leading off the hallways that surround the Great Hall. Depending on the case, an Edwardian divorce trial could pack the courtroom and the halls adjoining. It could occupy up to several weeks or be concluded in a matter of minutes. Judgment rendered or court adjourned, sublimity collapsed into ridicule or pathos as members of the press dashed out to submit or telegraph their paragraphs, sketches, and/or photos to their respective newspapers in London and throughout England. (See Illustration 2.)

When C.F.G. Masterman, publishing *The Condition of England* in 1909, imagined some future historian trying to reconstruct Edwardian England from whatever documents had been preserved, he gloomily envisioned the scholar consulting Edwardian tabloids, specifically the Sunday newspapers. And what would the historian glean from those? The picture of a land turned violent and mad. Further, "the most insistent noise" that he or she would hear reverberating through the Sunday papers would be "the clicking of the huge machine of English justice" as it swept thieves and murderers off to

OPPOSITE: *2 Tabloid Coverage of the Divorce Court* (News of the World, *February 19, 1905: 6*).

prison and tore apart "couples once married in affection" (4). Bad enough that future generations might
perceive Edwardian England in this manner, but Edwardian readers themselves were gathering this view of
their own times. Masterman believed that "seven out of
ten" English men and women were getting their "sole
picture" of the world outside their own local lives from
the Sunday press (3–4).[3] Certainly the Sunday tabloids
were well circulated. On its masthead, *News of the World*
boasted sales of one million copies per week.[4] As Florence Bell, writing of working-class life in the manufacturing town of Middlesborough, tells it, the typical
Sunday pattern for a working-class family, or at least
for the man of the house, would be to buy one of the
Sunday papers (news agents were among the few busi-
nesses allowed open on Sunday), curl up in bed with it,
and spend a relaxed, amusing day (*At the Works* 145).[5]

Dramas of the Divorce Court

To turn to the Divorce Court Report in a Sunday paper
such as *The Umpire, News of the World, People, Lloyd's
Weekly News, Reynold's News,* or *The Dispatch,* one flips
forward to page five or six, having encountered on previous pages a melange of national and international
news; human interest stories ("Negro Chased by Greek
Accused of Wounding"); sporting news; a short story or
serialized novel accompanied by a detailed drawing; a
song lyric; a steady flow of advertisements; and reports
on the Royals. Significantly, the Divorce Court page, or
pages, is typically framed by gossip from the world of

the theater ("Stage Whispers" in *The Umpire*) and cases from the criminal courts. Following the Divorce Court Report may be more human interest stories and advertisements, puzzles, and advice columns—legal, horticultural, medical, zoological. Included in the last were tips for pet owners, for example, measures to take if your canary suffers from diarrhea.

The Divorce Court Report often opened with a puff on the tales to come.

Dramas of the Divorce Court

During the week a number of cases were disposed of expeditiously in the Divorce Court. Several of these cases were undefended. In one instance somewhat remarkable letters from a husband were read and the wife received her decree. Another wife told a story of ill treatment during the honeymoon. Among some of those who figured prominently were an actor, a dramatic agent, an army officer, and an art student. (*The Umpire,* April 29, 1906, 7)

Headlines, stories, and illustrations in the form of drawings or photos crowd the page. In the issue of *The Umpire* quoted above the reader is tempted by the following headlines, among others:

In at the Back Door
Followed by a Thrashing from the Husband

Student and Lady
Artist Who Drew with Irresistible Power

"I Will Make You Happy"
American Lady's Romance

"The Fighting Parson"
Manchester Comedian Gets Divorce

The most condensed of the tabloid divorce stories typically derive what punch they have from some play on
words or joke on the involved parties' names.

Cut Adrift

Peter Gorman, a stoker on H.M.S. *Renown,* now stationed at
Devonport, was doing duty on a home station when he tied
the knot with his wife in Penryn, Cornwall, in October
1898. Afterwards he was sent on H.M.S. *Blake* to Malta, on
a three years' commission. Out of a possible 3 pounds 5 shillings a month, he forwarded 3 pounds a month to his wife,
but this allowance he stopped when reports reflecting on her
conduct reached him. In March last the cruise ended, and he
returned to Devonport. His wife was then living with a sailor
named Cyril Dove, and had borne a child in his absence. The
couple were stated to be now living together at Kearn, Devonport, and the judge ordered the matrimonial hawser which
held Mr. and Mrs. Gorman together to be cut. (*News of the
World,* February 19, 1905, 6)

A Printer's Error

Mr. Justice Deane granted a decree to Mr. James A. Percy
of Moss Side, Manchester, who asked for a divorce from

his wife on the ground of her adultery with Samuel Jones, at 24 Bristol Street, Hulme. The petitioner, a printer's foreman, was married in April, 1902, at Moss Side. They afterwards lived at Moss Side until respondent took to drink, and left her husband. It subsequently transpired that respondent was living with the corespondent in Manchester. (*The Umpire,* April 29, 1906, 7)

Case No. 30

Tilly *v.* Tilly, before Mr. Justice Bargrave Deane, which was about the 30th case he had heard during the sittings, was undefended in divorce court. Emily Charlotte married Mr. Tilly on October 15, 1888, at Warminster, but he left her to live with a lady of the unusual name of Spittle. Three little Spittles were the result of the latter union. Mrs. Tilly asked to be severed from her spouse on the grounds of desertion and adultery. *Decree nisi* with costs was granted. (*The Umpire,* January 14, 1906, 5)

A tale headlined MISS SHERLOCK HOLMES/HOW HER VISIT AT HOTEL WAS REWARDED finds interest in the fact that the private detective hired by the petitioner was a woman (*The Umpire,* January 14, 1906, 5).

The cumulative effect of these anecdotes, running on average between 80 and 250 words, is to suggest that divorce is a comical business, deserving a snicker. The very format, as tale follows tale down the page, reinforces the sense that these people are much of a piece, and not a very nice piece at that. A further effect, as Masterman suggests, is to give the misleading impression that divorce in England was a constant occurrence.

The slightly more developed tales, averaging between 600 and 850 words, appeal to reader interest by including especially scandalous details from the evidence and/or by quoting passages from intimate correspondence. THAT IS ENOUGH/HALIFAX MAN AND HIS WIFE opens with a characteristically packed sentence: "That Frank Rouse, of Halifax, was no fit associate for his wife, Mrs. Edith Mary Florence Rouse, now living at Damewood, Leamington, was perfectly obvious when the latter petitioned for a divorce against the former on the ground of his desertion and adultery." The story goes on to describe Mr. Rouse's drinking, his attempts "to brain" Mrs. Rouse "with a whiskey bottle," and his cursing her for not being a prostitute and thereby bringing some money into the house. As the presentation of evidence promised to continue, Judge Bargrave Deane apparently interrupted with "That is enough, *decree nisi* granted" (*The Umpire,* January 14, 1906, 5). As do many of these medium-length tales, MOTHER-IN-LAW'S DISCOVERY/DECREE GRANTED AGAINST A SOLICITOR draws the reader in with an opening letter.

My dear George, It is true I came to your flat as an uninvited guest, but whether fortunately or unfortunately I do not know. In looking for my daughter's workbasket in the drawing room, I accidentally came across some woman's underclothing of coarse material. As the mother of your wife, I was in duty bound to make an investigation of how they came there and what it all means. It must have been put there the two nights your wife was away, the Thursday and Friday before Easter. Your letter above shows you were sleeping at the flat on these days. . . . What am I to think? T. Wooloot (*News of the World,* January 22, 1905, 6) [ellipsis in original]

The still longer accounts, occupying two or three full columns and averaging between 3,000 and 4,000 words —that is, twelve to sixteen double-spaced typed pages— tend to downplay the reporter's wit, multiply the headlines, give more background regarding the parties, and include still more letters. In addition, these accounts offer descriptions of the parties and lengthy quotations from the testimony.[6] With more space, the reporter has a chance to develop a sustained tone for the piece. The stylistic options seem clear: pathos or humor.

One typical longer story starts off with a three-line header—WIFE AS DECOY/TERRIBLE REVELATIONS IN DIVORCE CASE/BIGAMY TO GAIN HAPPINESS—and launches itself with "Seldom has a sadder story been told in the Divorce Court than that narrated by Mrs. Anna Northover whose life was so intensely unhappy that she once tried to end her existence in order to escape the cruelties and indignities which her husband heaped upon her" (*News of the World,* January 16, 1910, 10). Promising the reader that her story "makes remarkable reading," the reporter proceeds to give a detailed summary of the opening tale constructed by the prosecution, Mr. Barnard, K.C. We read of Mr. Northover's refusing to ply his trade as a horse dealer and of his forcing his wife to go with him to Picadilly and Burlington Arcade. There he made her pick up gentlemen and invite them to visit her the following evening at the Northover residence. The scam involved Mr. Northover's subsequently greeting the men at the house and blackmailing them. However, between Anna Northover and one gentleman a genuine relationship developed. Using the eye-catching, embedded headline, the reporter's summary of Mr. Barnard's narrative continues:

When this gentleman called at the house, her husband admitted him to petitioner's room, where she was lying ill at the time, and left them together. Mr. Fraser, who was

Very Much in Love

with petitioner at the time, believing her to be single, proposed marriage to her, and she, being so unhappy with her husband that she had attempted to commit suicide, accepted him. (10)

Mr. Barnard goes on to tell of Anna Northover's bigamous marriage to Mr. Fraser, Mr. Northover's appearance on the scene, Mr. Fraser's learning of her previous marriage, and his intent to stand by her. Mr. Northover then attempted to get money from the two of them, eventually charging Anna with bigamy. Evidence, including a long letter printed verbatim, is given respecting Mr. Northover's adultery, cruelty, and connivance in his wife's early misconduct. Mr. Barnard and Mr. Justice Bargrave Deane commence to discuss legal points, and then Mrs. Northover is called to the stand: "She is a tall, handsome, well-proportioned woman, with a profusion of fair hair. She was stylishly though quietly dressed. To a crowded court she told her very sad tale" (10). The story already told by Mr. Barnard is now repeated, this time in question-answer format.

After I told my husband about the marriage with Mr. Fraser, he said he would make Mr. Fraser pay. The next day Mr. Fraser came to the house.—What did he do?—He called my husband a scoundrel and

Knocked Him Down

Later in the day my husband made me sign a paper assigning to him everything that I had, and he told me to go to Mr. Fraser, and I went away with him. Judge: Were you all friendly together?—Mrs. Northover: There was no friendliness. I was terrified by my husband. (10)

Mrs. Northover's sister testifies, as does Mr. Fraser. Given that the case is undefended, Mr. Northover is never called. Eventually Mr. Justice Bargrave Deane pronounces judgment. He will use the discretion given to him under the law and disregard Mrs. Northover's bigamy. She will receive her decree. Follows then the denouement. He cannot, of course, acquit Anna Northover of treating Mr. Fraser with the most cruel deceit and finds that gentleman occupying an entirely innocent position in this case. At the same time, he would find it difficult to imagine a more miserable life than that which Mrs. Northover was forced to lead with her brutal and inhuman husband. He finds Alfred Northover guilty of cruelty and adultery. Petitioner is granted a *decree nisi* and custody of the couple's child.[7]

Foregrounded in the Northover story are scandal and misery; foregrounded in other examples of these more developed tales are scandal and sass. In the sassy stories, we encounter the same basic format as in the pathetic tales, but here the reporter highlights a witness's riposte, a couple's naughtiness, the courtroom's bursting into laughter. Reporting on the trial of Pritchard *v.* Pritchard, the writer opens with the headline—AMAZING DIVORCE PLOT/CRUELTY CAREFULLY STAGE-MANAGED/CROSS

PETITIONS DISMISSED—and tells of William Oscar Pritchard and his wife, Margarite Anne Pritchard, colluding in their efforts to get a divorce. At one point they staged a "cruelty" scene:

> [Mr. Pritchard] said Mr. Dutton and a young lady had tea with witness and his wife, and during the evening he went into the kitchen, where his wife had gone. "It was so funny that it was ten minutes before we could get on," he said, "but then I caught hold of my wife's arm while she screamed." (Laughter.) "The lady friend rushed in and saw the act, and that founded one of the charges of cruelty." (Loud laughter.) (*News of the World,* January 23, 1910, 10)

While there is evidence of much unhappiness in the entire Pritchard story, with letters and multiple versions of incidents of adultery and cruelty given on both sides, the keynote is comedy. Mr. Justice Bargrave Deane lectures all involved, elicits further laughter, and dismisses both petitions.

If one steps back and looks at these more developed short stories in general, one can see them employing the same stylistic formula used elsewhere in the Sunday paper. As historians of England's popular press have observed, by the middle of the nineteenth century, the mass circulation popular papers increasingly adopted a style Matthew Arnold in 1887 disparagingly dubbed the "new" journalism. Although, as Laurel Brake points out, neither the "old" nor the "new" journalism were in fact monolithic, new journalism came to be associated with sensationalism, the reporting of newsy items as opposed to weighty editorials, and a lively, readable style.[8] Be the topic a national debate over curriculum, the sinking of a fishing boat, a theft, or a divorce, the papers piqued curiosity with teasing headlines. Illustrations were amply provided; and such puns and word-play as could be devised were tucked in for added interest. The focus of the report was less on issues and more on the personalities of the people involved. Speaking specifically of Edwardian reports on divorce, an article in the *Morning Post* of September 29, 1910, summed up the conventions this way: The largest section of the public demanded "descriptive accounts deliberately written to excite and to interest. . . . To that end, all the resources of illustrations, personal anecdote, of descriptive paragraph, and of arresting headline are called into play" (quoted in *Report of the Royal Commission* 3:188). In addition, the divorce stories reflect their location in the paper's layout: They carry forward the voyeuristic tenor of the preceding page's theatrical gossip while glancing ahead to the pathos and sensationalism of the crime reports. Writing of the similar crime-story style adopted by the French popular press, Berenson points out the contradictory emotions elicited: Readers are invited to feel shock at the deeds described, a degree of fascination with the guilty parties, sympathy with the victims, and a secret relief, perhaps smugness, that all of this has happened to someone else (211).

Members of the press who testified before the Royal Commission on Divorce were generally in favor of modifying the style in which divorce trials were reported. But most argued against any proposal that would do away with publicity altogether, or even radically curb it. I indicate at the close of this chapter the many arguments that were mounted in support of the current practice, but a key one to mention here is the principle of open courts. A judicial system that was open to the public, in person and by way of the press, was seen as a hallmark of English justice. Open courts were essential to protecting the people on trial and educating the public regarding the law and its practices. With reference to the second rationale, the shorter divorce stories obviously did little to educate readers about divorce law and procedures. A longer tale, such as the Northover story, began that process, organizing its narrative in a way that reflected the sequence of a trial's stages. The divorce story that had the greatest potential for carrying out this educative task, however, was the genuinely long tale, the one that received front-page coverage for weeks on end. Like a modern-day television camera, the reporter's gaze ranged over the courtroom day after day, introduced and then followed the principals throughout the trial, recorded the many moves and countermoves of the prosecution and defense, and closed with the climactic judgment and denouement. As we have become increasingly aware, this kind of extended, intimate court report has great potential to demystify the routine practice of justice and, at the very same time, to theatricalize beyond all human recognition every person and issue it touches.

Stirling *v.* Stirling

When Edwardians cited egregious instances of divorce trial publicity, they often spoke of the Stirling trial.[9] Although the trial was held in Edinburgh, many of the principals and all of the witnesses were English. The ingredients for sensation were there from the outset as members of England's upper class flung accusations of adultery in high places, from Paris to London, from the Henley Regatta to the Isle of Wight. If the premise of this chapter is granted—that the reigning narrative on Edwardian divorce was primarily constructed and maintained through the peculiar English conjunction of imposing trial and widespread publicity—then a trial such as Stirling *v.* Stirling can be seen as doing yeoman's labor in that educative task. (See Illustration 3.) Hearings in the case opened on Tuesday, January 19, 1909, and adjourned on Monday, February 15, 1909. Judgment was postponed until March 10. The judge in the case was Lord Guthrie, who would soon be serving as one of the commissioners on the forthcoming Royal Commission on Divorce and Matrimonial Causes.

In paper after paper, the basic plot was laid out in the following terms: Mrs. Clara Elizabeth Stirling, twenty-four, formerly Miss Taylor of New York and at one time a member of the "Cozy Corner" girls in the musical comedy *The Earl and the Girl,* now residing at a hotel in Jermyn Street, London, was petitioning for a divorce from Mr. John Alexander Stirling, twenty-eight, of Kippendavie, a Perthshire laird, former lieutenant in the 3rd Scots Guards, and current resident of Chesham Street, London. Her charge: his misconduct with Mrs. Mabel Louise Atherton, thirty-four, resident of Amberley

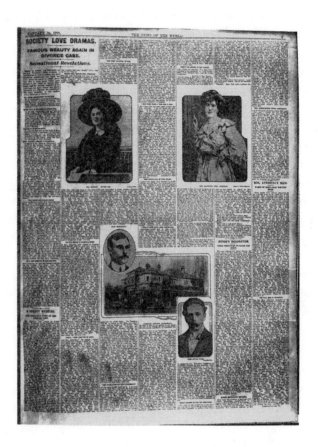

Cottage, Maidenhead, daughter of Sir Edward Dean-Paul, sister of the present baronet, and the divorced wife of Colonel T. J. Atherton.[10] Readers were reminded that Mrs. Atherton's name had been before them previously in association with a breach of promise suit she had brought in 1906 against the corespondent named in her divorce, Captain the Honorable J.R.L. Yarde-Buller. Mr. Stirling, however, taking the position of the wronged husband, had filed a counterpetition, alleging misconduct between Mrs. Stirling and Viscount Northland, twenty-seven, only son and heir of the Earl of Ranfurly, and currently a captain in the Yorkshire Dragoons.[11]

Readers encountering the first installment of the tale in *The Umpire* on Sunday, January 24, were greeted with two introductions. The lead story, featured on page one, gave the most up-to-date information, covering the previous day's testimony by Mabel Atherton. The story on page nine then backtracked to the actual opening of the trial five days before. For Atherton's testimony, the headlines were stacked four deep.

Beautiful Woman's Admissions

Must I Answer, My Lord?

Mrs. Atherton Gives Evidence
in Society Divorce Case

Her Strenuous Denials

OPPOSITE: *3 Report on the Stirling Trial*
(News of the World, *January 24, 1909: 9*).

The scene is set. We read of crowds surrounding the buildings and of Lord Guthrie moving the trial out of the large High Court to a much smaller courtroom at the extreme east end of the complex. Police stand guard barring entrance to all but official personages and the press. Taking the stand, Mrs. Atherton draws "murmurs of general interest." She is tall, fascinating, slender. "Her dark brown velvet Directoire costume suited her to perfection, especially when her wealth of dark chestnut brown hair was set off by a black fur toque, with a huge white feather aigrette and some dull amber pins at her throat. At the back was a large rosette of pink and heliotrope ribbon, which stood out against her dark sable stole" (1).[12] Responding to sympathetic questions from Mr. Clyde, K.C., who is acting for Mr. Stirling, she moves through her account of what happened. The reader, who is entering this tale very much in media res, has reason to be confused but intrigued. Mrs. Atherton's story serves as a prelude, full of teasing notes. We gather for example that Atherton's former maid, Mlle. Therese Dagonne, had testified against her earlier in the week. But, asks Mr. Clyde, is Mlle. Dagonne's testimony reliable? Did you not fire her after discovering that she had stolen fifty pairs of new gloves from you? Did she not say she would make you suffer for that? Did she not get her present employment through the influence of Lord Northland? Were you not Clara Stirling's good friend? Were not you and Jack Stirling simply pals? Yes, yes, yes, responds Mabel Atherton.

When Mr. Shaw, K.C., acting for Mrs. Stirling, takes over, an altogether different set of questions is posed. You said you were thirty-four; are you not actually thirty-eight? Were you not divorced by Colonel

Atherton? Did you not commit adultery with Captain
Yarde-Buller? Here Mrs. Atherton turns to Lord Guthrie, "Must I answer, my Lord?" He says she must.
Then, yes, yes, yes, she answers. Ostracized from decent society and following your former ways, did you
not misconduct yourself with Jack Stirling in Paris,
your cottage at Maidenhead, the Stirling home on
Chesham Street, and the Ocean Hotel on the Isle of
Wight? No, no, no.

If this initial introduction in what will turn out to be a
very long narrative is working, the reader is scan-
dalized, amused, and eager to start putting all of these
notes together into a coherent story. Who did what,
where, when, why? We turn to page nine for our second
introduction. Again, the headlines are stacked.

Society Divorce Drama

Laird and the Lord

Confessions and Accusations from High Life

The Beautiful Lady

The scene is set once more as the key witness to start off
this segment, Mrs. Clara Stirling, is introduced: "When
Mrs. Stirling stepped into the witness box the courtroom was crowded, for the interest in the society divorce suit was intense. She is a particularly handsome
woman with an Edna May face and hair and something
of the demure American accent which made Edna May
famous. She was wearing a black velvet dress, furs, and

a large black 'Merry Widow' hat. Her face, pale when she commenced her story, regained its color and she became very apt in some of her replies to counsel" (9). Again we are instructed as to the charges in these countersuits. As Mrs. Stirling begins her tale under the guidance of her advocate, Mr. Shaw, K.C., we learn that her marriage with Jack had begun in secret, owing to the opposition of the Stirling family. Still, all had gone well, with a son, Pat, born in 1907. Then Mrs. Atherton arrived on the scene. Mrs. Stirling's first suspicions of a possible affair between Jack and Mabel occurred during a weekend trip to Paris. The party had comprised Mabel, Jack, Clara, and Jack's long-time friend, Lord Northland. But Mrs. Stirling's fondness for Mabel Atherton kept struggling against her fears. She considered Mabel a true friend. The suspicions nevertheless increased on subsequent occasions, for example on one of the nights Mabel stayed as a houseguest at the Stirling home in Chesham Street and at the Henley Regatta when Mabel and Jack went off together in one of the boats. Suspicion crystallized into certainty when Clara, in America visiting her mother, received a letter from Pat's nurse. Nurse Morris wrote that Mr. Stirling, Mrs. Atherton, and Mrs. Atherton's child had left together for the Ocean Hotel on the Isle of Wight. Clara immediately returned to London, only to find them all back from the Isle of Wight and Mrs. Atherton ensconced in Clara's very own bedroom. She, Clara, could stand no more, moved out, sought out Lord Northland for help and friendship, and now begs the court for relief.

So goes Clara Stirling's opening tale. Mr. Shaw steps back and Mr. Clyde begins the cross-examination. He asks Clara about her life in the theater before her marriage, emphasizing her free and easy ways and her own friendship with Lord Northland before her marriage. He draws forth from her a far less happy history of the early years of the Stirling marriage, including bitter quarrels over money. She pertly admits to extravagance, and we read of laughter in the court. And then Mr. Clyde produces two key letters. In the first, to Lord Northland, Clara comments on how kind Jack is being about all of this, asks if Lord Northland truly cares for her, and confesses to her own deep feelings for him. In the second, written subsequently to Jack, Clara says, "Go ahead and divorce me. I won't fight it." When Mrs. Stirling tries to explain these letters, she says that the letter to Lord Northland was just a way of talking. The letter to Jack was written after she had left the Chesham Street house. She wanted all of this over and thought that the easiest route was for him to divorce her, simply on the grounds of her desertion. In no way was she admitting to adultery.

Mr. Shaw now steps back in to repair whatever damage has been done. Mainly, he gets Mrs. Stirling to give details respecting one of the occasions upon which she alleges adultery took place between Mabel and Jack and to bemoan the fact that she did not hoard incriminating letters as others in this case seem to have done. Her witnesses are then called, from Nurse Morris, to the chambermaid at the Ocean Hotel, to Mabel's former maid, Therese Dagonne.

Mrs. Stirling's presentation of evidence is completed by midday Thursday, January 21. Mr. Stirling then takes the stand, at this point simply to defend himself against the charges made against him. We read nothing of his costume or appearance but learn that he speaks in a conversational tone, unless to emphasize a point. He rehearses his view of his marriage with Clara, detailing his financial straits, his concerted efforts to get the family back into decent financial shape, and her lack of understanding or sense of responsibility. He admits that he had been sleeping apart from Clara, in his own dressing room, mainly because she did not seem to want relations with him and insisted on reading until two o'clock in the morning. Her reading habits were far from convenient for him, given that he had to get up early to go to work every morning. Their sleeping apart had occurred before either of them had made the acquaintance of Mrs. Atherton. Throughout his opening statement, Jack Stirling argues that he and Mabel were friends, as were Mabel and Clara, and that Clara had never expressed any concern over him and Mabel until the divorce petition against her and Lord Northland was drawn up. At that point, Mr. Stirling maintained, Clara saw the potential damage to herself and began to doubt Lord Northland's commitment to her. Then and only then did the charge of adultery between himself and Mabel Atherton enter the case.

As this first long installment from the January 24 edition of *The Umpire* comes to a close, we are promised that Mr. Stirling's story will be continued next week as he answers the specific charges brought against him, incident by incident. But first, Lord de la Warr has requested a chance to respond publicly to allegations made against him by Therese Dagonne regarding his relations with Mabel Atherton. Let the record show that he had not been named as a corespondent in Atherton's earlier divorce case. Admittedly, he had given her shelter when she had come to him, highly distraught over the news of

Captain Yarde-Buller's marriage, but that was the extent of his involvement. To round out the week's testimony, readers are invited to turn back to page one and reread Mrs. Atherton's testimony.

The narrative complexities in this one installment are repeated on three subsequent Sundays, from January 31 through February 14, as every principal presents his or her statement, is then cross-examined, reexamined by her or his advocate, and as witnesses are called to testify and are cross-examined. Subplots proliferate, inviting a paraphrase of George Eliot's advice: All you need for a good divorce story is two couples in a small town. The small town here is aristocratic London. The divorce story develops a thousand aspects as each side constructs stories to refute the opposition. Both sides drag in material evidence whenever possible: an elaborate model of Amberley Cottage where misconduct did or did not take place between Clara and Lord Northland or between Mabel and Jack; the lock that had been on the door to the bathroom at the Stirling's Chesham Street house and either was or was not in working order on one of the nights Mabel Atherton spent as a house guest; additional letters, including a passionate one from Lord Northland to Clara, and a desperate one, threatening suicide, from Clara to Lord Northland.

Lord Northland, one notes, was not called to testify until Wednesday, February 3. Coverage of the trial within the Sunday papers for February 7 was somewhat down in general, making his actual testimony less of a feature than that of the other three principals. On that Sunday, in fact, more attention is given to the fact that Mrs. Stirling's barrister is returning his brief to take a governmental appointment. Coverage again picks up on February 14, as the papers report closing testimony and the summarizing speeches of each side in each suit.

Climax is achieved with Lord Guthrie's judgment, delivered on March 10: Mrs. Stirling is found guilty of adultery with Lord Northland; Mr. Stirling is acquitted of allegations of adultery with Mabel Atherton. Mr. Stirling wins the divorce and gets custody of Pat. Lord Guthrie will hear arguments respecting costs and access to the child. But the narrative is still not over. Lord Guthrie must now shift from the position of listener to storyteller. He must deliver the all-important denouement.

First, this trial has taken much too long—"eighteen days in all—equal in hours to a Scottish University Winter Session" (*The London Times,* March 11, 1909, 4). Not that he is recommending a return to dueling, but, in the past, such a case would have been settled in a half an hour with weapons in the woods. He then moves back and forth between evaluations of the evidence and of the lives of the parties.

Looking at the evidence, he foregrounds a decision made by Clara Stirling's advocates in their summing up of her case, as well as the letters she and Lord Northland wrote. Lord Guthrie notes that in the barristers' summing up, Mrs. Stirling's advocate decided to drop all charges of Mr. Stirling's being with Mrs. Atherton anywhere but at the Ocean Hotel at Sandown on the Isle of Wight. This would suggest that the testimony of Nurse Morris and Therese Dagonne, respecting misconduct in Paris, Amberley Cottage, or the Chesham Street house, had collapsed. As for adultery in the Ocean Hotel, comments Lord Guthrie, Sandown was at the height of the busy summer season. Mabel Atherton had her young son with her. There is much evidence that she loves this child and wants Colonel Atherton to continue to allow her to see him. Further, the son, an active, high-spirited boy, often slept in a twin bed in the same room or was in an adjoining room with the door open. Taken with other evidence, it seems unlikely that Mr. Stirling was sleeping with Mabel Atherton in her room at the Ocean Hotel as alleged. As for the letters, Lord Guthrie believed that they, along with other evidence, indicated an affair between Clara Stirling and Lord Northland.

Moving to the characters of the four principals, Lord Guthrie finds that all have been leading the most idle and selfish of lives. "In their attitude towards human life there was not much to choose between the players in this squalid drama. All four, Scottish laird, American ex-actress, Peer's son, and divorcee, appeared to have looked upon life merely as an opportunity for having a good time, regardless of their duty to themselves, to each other, to their children, and to their relatives, and indifferent to the good opinion of self-respecting people" (*The London Times,* March 11, 1909, 4). In constructing an explanation for Mrs. Stirling's behavior in particular, he reads her as an inherently unstable, undisciplined, extravagant person who ended up in this country with no real support from family or respectable friends. He chastises her for laziness and restlessness. She stayed in bed until noon. She gadded about. She separated herself from husband and child. She broke up her home. Mrs. Atherton, for all of her beauty and graciousness, seemed similarly restless and adrift, owing to her previous divorce and current bohemian style of living. Neither woman seemed endowed with common sense, taste, or intelligence, but certainly Clara Stirling was the more culpable. Mr. Stirling is criticized for stepping outside his class in marrying someone from the chorus line of the Adelphi and, having done so, with failing to guide his wife with sufficient firmness toward the position she should have held. Lord Northland's behavior—especially his treachery to his host and friend Jack Stirling—could only be explained by "sexual passion not under control," the kind of "passion which had made of some of the most chivalrous characters in history, sacred and profane, not only adulterers, but liars and murderers to boot" (*The London Times,* March 11, 1909, 4).

As Lord Guthrie tries to imagine how all of this could have been prevented, he fails to envision some structural problem at the heart of this failed marriage. In his view, whatever went wrong has nothing to do with the way marriage was envisioned during this period and everything to do with the characters of the parties involved. Things would have gone better if Lord Northland had been less passionate; if Mr. Stirling had been firmer; if Mrs. Atherton had shown more discretion, now and in the past; and if Mrs. Stirling had somehow been endowed with a less ungovernable temper and a greater sense of responsibility. Case dismissed.[13]

The aim of this chapter is to present the decade's reigning narrative on divorce. Criticism of that narrative forms the subject of Chapters 2 and 3. However, I want to wrestle here with what may seem obvious: The possibility that Clara Stirling did not receive justice, that the courtroom procedures muffled her. That possibility in turn slides toward the generalization that Edwardian wives in general were ill-served by the formal trial, with its all-male cast and patriarchal script. As I note in the

Introduction, however, Edwardian wives did better in the divorce court than did their husbands, though both did very well. As for Clara Stirling's experience, Anne Bottomley forces us to ask some tough questions regarding formal trials and power dynamics. Arguing that formal trials may, in fact, have real advantages for the less powerful person in a dispute, Bottomley points out that a formal trial gives each disputant substantive rights, procedural safeguards, and a lawyer trained to mitigate the power imbalances that exist in the culture at large. In thinking realistically about how Clara Stirling fared, we need to ask "relative to what other process?" and "relative to whom?" Would a less formal procedure—say mediation—have worked better for her? Possibly not. Clara Stirling was an outsider with little money of her own. Ranked against her were lords, ladies, and earls. We do not know who was telling the truth at this trial, but it seems fair to say that Clara had a better chance to construct her version of reality within this procedure than any other available.

As for the question, "relative to whom?" if Clara Stirling lost, Mabel Atherton was among the winners. Rightly or wrongly, the process validated Mabel's explanation of what had happened. She—whom the culture could easily brand as an older, scheming, sensual woman, a fallen mother, a divorcee still leading a shameless life—was believed.

Bottomley's recent defense of formal judicial procedures was written in the context of an increasing number of divorce cases in England being decided through informal mediation procedures. But her argument also speaks to an important current debate within feminist legal theory in America, one that pits a "rule of law" approach to adjudication against a "storytelling" approach.[14] Applied to the situation of Clara Stirling, the storytelling approach would say that the formalized rationality of the trial made it difficult for Clara adequately to convey the context of her actions, the individual circumstances of her situation, and her own perceptions of what happened. Simultaneously, as "a legal habit of thinking" (Schepple 2084), the formal trial encouraged Lord Guthrie to suppress any empathy he might have felt for Clara Stirling, the outsider in this case.

To the contrary, argue advocates of the rule of law approach. The formal procedures of the trial probably protected Mrs. Stirling more than they inhibited her. Insiders—Jack Stirling for example—are just as prone to tell stories, and theirs will often be the more believable to the judge or jury. In many cases, argues Toni Massaro, it is only by invoking the dispassionate rule of law that hegemonic tales can be interrupted. She cites the value of curtailing storytelling in the case of a rape victim with a questionable sexual history. Following Massaro's reasoning, one can imagine a less formal procedure making much more of Clara Stirling's life before marriage, or indeed of Mabel Atherton's previous affairs.

I return to the dynamics of the Stirling trial in general by asking, what did all of this accomplish? For Edwardians, the question split into two concerns: What did the adversarial trial accomplish in cases of divorce and what was the value of this kind of extensive press coverage? Reformists, whose criticisms and counterstories constitute much of Chapters 2 and 3, felt that the open and adversarial trial was barbaric, something one would not

expect to see in a civilized country. E.S.P. Haynes
quotes the passionate denunciation of one visitor, who
published her reactions in the *Evening Times:* "Men and
women who are dragged to the Divorce Court are unhappy, shipwrecked people. They require sympathy
and understanding, and instead they are made the
quarry of the mob. . . . I sat in Court, and as I heard the
attempts made to put the worst constructions on the
most innocent of things I could have torn the skin off
my face. . . . I thought I must be living three hundred
years back, in the days when they burned witches."[15]
Haynes himself goes on to criticize press coverage. It
is the Puritan who supports widespread publicity, he
writes. From it, the Puritan gains two distinct kinds of
pleasure: first, the enjoyment of scandalous reading and,
second, the enjoyment of knowing that pain and humiliation are being visited upon people who have strayed
from the paths of convention ("The Publicity of Divorce" 146).

But for other Edwardians, the conjunction of this
kind of trial and this kind of coverage made a great deal
of sense. In their view, this very English blend did educate the public on the workings of the law and effectively maintained the reigning views on marriage and
divorce. To credit this perspective, one can make the
following argument: As current legal theorists suggest,
the kind of coverage the Stirling trial received does in
fact represent much of what goes on in the courtroom.
In *Reconstructing Reality in the Courtroom,* W. Lance Bennett and Martha S. Feldman characterize the dynamics
of the courtroom in Western culture as essentially narrative in nature.[16] Nothing, they contend, so aptly describes the entire process, from beginning to end, than

the concept of narrative messiness and sprawl. "Readers" of a trial, from judge and jury to interested parties of all kinds, are confronted with narratives "replete with multiple points of view, subplots, time lapses, missing information, and ambiguous clues" (5). How do these readers make sense of the discrepant information they are given? Much the way readers of any narrative text do, including narratives as low-brow as a report in *The Umpire:* They make a series of connections—empirical, linguistic, logical, normative, and aesthetic—and then shape the sundry narratives into the most coherent overarching plot they can construct (67). They make a story out of stories. And here, Gerald Lopez's concept of stock stories is helpful.

Defining a trial as a "remedial ceremony"—a ceremony designed to bring about a remedy—Lopez argues that the key activity in the ceremony is the negotiating of "stock stories." Stock stories have been variously called scripts or schemas. Regardless of what term is preferred, they are the familiar narratives we use daily to help us understand and make decisions about our own or others' experiences. Why are stock stories privileged in a trial? According to Lopez, time is an issue. A judge cannot sit on a case forever. Important too is the nature of the remedial ceremony's expected finale: In a Western courtroom, the ceremony must come to certain meaning in certain terms. Generally it must produce clear winners and losers, often resulting in a "winner takes all" solution. There is, in addition, the adjudicator's need to be seen as legitimate by the community, by both peers and public. All of these factors, contends Lopez, will encourage a judge to downplay any uncertainty, to reject unusual stories as demanding too much time for reflection and investigation, and to discount the tale that least accords with the community's norms. To a large degree, the judge will go with whatever stock story, in the context of the trial, is most familiar and conventional with respect to the mores of the community. Such is certainly the path Lord Guthrie took as he constructed his clear and conventional tale about hardworking husbands, passionate young men, and shameful, undisciplined wives.

To recognize the mesh between the trial's narrative dynamics and the long tabloid report is again to affirm the contention that such coverage did educate Edwardian readers in the ways of the law, at least as the law was realized on occasions of adjudication. To recognize further that the trials and their tabloid coverage tended to produce and reproduce stock stories is to grant the contention that this English practice was designed to maintain the reigning narrative on marriage and divorce. Edwardians taking this view were in fact anticipating an argument Clifford Geertz made in his Storrs lecture at Yale in 1981, an argument richly elaborated by legal theorists throughout the 1980s: Laws should not be thought of as discrete commands; rather, they are a way of imagining the real. Laws and legal processes tell stories.[17] In the case of Edwardian divorce law and practice, the overarching story told by trial and tabloid went as follows: At the heart of the story are two ideals, lifelong fidelity for England's married citizens and open, evenhanded justice for England's courts.

As stated in the Church of England marriage service, the purpose of marriage is to help people fulfill their earthly duties: to have children; to direct and channel their sexual energies in ways helpful rather than harmful to the community; and to love another human and make sacrifices for him or her. One reward for fulfilling these duties is the avoidance of public humiliation. Marriage should begin with the consent of each partner and in creaturely love; but with or without lasting love, it should continue out of a sense of fidelity to the solemn promise one made upon marriage, a promise to oneself, one's partner, the nation, and God. One's happiness, day to day, year to year, is simply not the issue. As the words of Jesus indicate, the one act that dissolves this otherwise indissoluble and sacred union of man, woman, and God is adultery. It wrecks havoc on the union. The adultery of the husband does not so clearly destroy the very foundations of the marriage but it may, with one other grievous offense, serve as a ground for dissolution.[18]

In coming to the court with a petition to divorce, one is begging the state to dissolve a legal contract and unbind a holy sacrament for two reasons: because of one's unbearable suffering and because the alleged acts of adultery have already dissolved the union. A grievous matrimonial offense has been committed. The guilty party must be punished by being deprived of home, spouse, children, money. The innocent must be relieved. There can be no suggestion that both parties desire this dissolution or that the petitioner has committed any offenses him- or herself. For if either were true, the rest of the plot falls apart. No one would be innocent. No one would be punished. Rather than the state reluctantly going against its deep commitment to marital stability out of its concern for a suffering citizen, the couple (either as colluders or guilty people) would be facing the state together against the state's interest.

Finally, getting at the truth of what did happen may not be easy, but tried and true legal procedures will work. Through the techniques of adversarial law, carried out by highly trained people, who are necessarily men, the history of this marriage can be discovered and fairly judged. If the process is expensive, that is ultimately to the good. The last thing the nation needs is cheap and easy divorce.

Respecting publicity, advocates cited the deterrence effect; the punishment of the guilty; the vindication of the innocent; and again England's commitment to open courts. In the Royal Commission Hearings, witnesses from the press spoke eloquently to the deterrence issue. The members of the press related how people would continually come to them, hoping to keep their divorce story out of the papers, how they would beg, weep, offer bribes. Fortunately, the papers could not and did not respond. If one paper did not publicize the story, countless others would. Publicity also serves as a deterrent to blackmail. If trial reports existed but were kept secret, any amount of blackmail could occur as people with access to those records pursued the vulnerable parties (*Report of the Royal Commission* 3:177).

On a different issue, the publicizing of divorce is crucial to the punishing of the guilty and the vindicating of the innocent. Who divorced whom, for what reasons, what the arguments were, how long it took the judge to decide and how he summed it all up: The entire story helps the innocent party go forward and face the community; condemns the guilty; and gives fair warning to any future parties who may have dealings with the principals.

But perhaps most important, as noted above, English courts had prided themselves for centuries on their openness—no star chambers here. A free press was seen as an essential guard to individual liberty. Nor was the openness of the courts an issue solely involving the press. Except in extraordinary cases, the public in all of its scruffiness must be able to walk in off the streets and listen to whatever the trial brings forth.

According to the reigning narrative, the Edwardian way of conducting and publicizing divorce trials served the community's interests in obvious ways. Stable marriages channel sexual energies, allow children to be born and supported through private rather than public funds, and insure national productivity through a proper division of labor between men and women. Because so much community good rides on conjugal stability, the state will try hard to prevent any marriage from being dissolved. With trials and tabloids as the means, it will make that dissolution frightening, expensive, public, and humiliating.

The next two chapters examine the volley of counter-stories launched at this dominant narrative by reform-minded Edwardians, as well as the stock stories that were mounted in defense. Cannot a story about failed marriage be about something other than sex? Cannot the people involved be seen through lenses that neither trivialize nor theatricalize their lives? Might not there be a reconfigured cast of official listeners at the trial, one that is not so unrelentingly masculine? Is the adultery of a wife truly different from that of a husband? Must the price of admission into the courtroom be so high? Must the tale be framed by scripture? Must the disaffected spouses approach the court as sworn adversaries? Are the principals in fact only the husband and wife? What about children? Surely in telling stories about the dissolving of marriage, there is more to be said and other ways of saying it.

Counterstories:
The Royal Commission on Divorce and Matrimonial Causes

Dear Lady Balfour,

Seeing in to-day's paper that you are one of the Commission on Divorce laws I shall take the liberty of writing you and ask if anything could be done for me. My husband deserted me 4 years ago and resides in Mexico. He is I know living with a woman out there as man and wife. He never sends me a penny neither does he keep his children. . . . I cannot get my divorce simply because it is far more than I can ever save out of my earnings. . . . I do not come under the "pauper" law having a bisiness [sic], although all my furniture is hire and I have not any money of my own except what I earn. Can you possibly help the really poor yet decent woman who could pay a little to get her case, but not the fearful and impossible sum that is required now. . . .

Thanking you in hopes,

Yours faithfully,

—*Report of the Royal Commission on Divorce and Matrimonial Causes* 4, appendix 26:173 [The letters were printed anonymously]

The above letter to Lady Frances Balfour challenges the reigning narrative on divorce in a number of ways. Like hundreds of others sent to members of the Royal Commission, it forces the reader to ask what is meant by the concept of indissoluble marriage. Is this woman's marriage not already dissolved? Would not a divorce at this point simply recognize the fact? Equally important, the letter demands some explanation for the prohibitive cost of getting a divorce. The writer has the necessary grounds, adultery and desertion, but not the necessary cash. The reigning narrative may uphold an ideal of lifelong marriage but it also upholds an ideal of justice to all English citizens. What kind of justice is this? In addition, the letter introduces the possibility of a woman bringing her legal concerns to another woman, a theme that repeatedly comes up in the Royal Commission hearings. And finally, it challenges a general perception, current then and now, that women of the working class were monolithic in their disapproval of divorce.

Lopez concludes his analysis of the remedial ceremonies that tend to produce stock stories with a lament: "Must we inevitably repeat ourselves?" (60). Cannot even a conventional remedial ceremony trade in something other than received wisdom? Yes, responds Delgado. Specifically interested in legal solutions to racial conflicts, Delgado celebrates the power and presence of counterstories. Capable of unsettling the mindsets of the powerful, counterstories can "quicken and enlarge consciences"; "they can show that what we believe is ridiculous, self-serving, or cruel"; and they are most often told by members of an outgroup (2415, 2438).[1]

What kinds of remedial ceremonies might be especially open to counterstories? Recalling Lopez we can infer that they will be ceremonies that do not work within narrow time constraints nor are obliged to suppress uncertainty. They need not come to closure with one winner, one loser. They will be ceremonies, I suggest, very like the hearings conducted by the Royal Commission on Divorce and Matrimonial Causes. The aim of this chapter is to examine the ways in which the commission, meeting as it did over a period of approx-

imately three years and expressing in its final report
England's agreements and disagreements on divorce
law reform, challenged the reigning narrative and stock
stories produced by the Edwardian trial and tabloid.

In staging a lengthy ceremony designed to recommend remedies for perceived problems in England's
divorce law and custom, the Royal Commission on Divorce not only had *time* to elicit and study counterstories, it had a mandate to do so. What is a marriage? What
constitutes marital failure? How should the community
address such failure? As the Asquith government had
conceded in appointing the commission, conventional
answers no longer convinced. In the end, the commissioners recommended reducing the cost of divorce,
establishing equity between men and women, and curbing publicity.[2] They split on the question of broadening
grounds beyond adultery. (Appendix I summarizes the
commission's recommendations and indicates when
those recommendations were acted upon.) But also "in
the end," the English had subjected themselves to an
extraordinary exchange of tales on marital desire gone
awry. In the phrasing of Peter Brooks, through narrative, they had entered into the woods of their anxieties;
spent time in that shadowy place voicing fears, dreams,
longings, and ambivalence; and emerged with fuller understanding.[3]

The listeners in this chapter are primarily the fourteen
commissioners, best seen as a group of policy analysts
warranted by King Edward to solicit a range of stories
on an issue of high uncertainty and recommend changes
in the law. Beyond them, however, stands the vast
reading public, who, by all accounts, closely followed
these highly publicized hearings. The tellers comprise

the 246 witnesses who came to testify, as well as those who wrote letters and/or sent their tales forward through a representative. I take as my focus one especially interesting narrative exchange. The chapter closes with an attempt to evaluate the storytelling that went on in this arena. What issues were and were not aired? Who won? Who lost? What was accomplished?

Commissioners and Witnesses

The appointment of the commission was announced on November 10, 1909. With his sixteen years of experience in the Divorce Division of the High Court and his controversial judgment in the Dodd case, Gorell Barnes, now Lord Gorell, headed the commission and helped to shape it. Breaking with tradition, he insisted that this commission would include women. As long time social activist and suffragist Lady Balfour recalled, women had never before served on a Royal Commission looking into family law issues, and rarely on ones looking into any other subject. King Edward had initially objected, thinking divorce "not a subject where women's opinions could be conveniently expressed." Backing up Lord Gorell, Prime Minister Asquith argued "that as women were equally concerned with men in the Divorce Courts they could hardly be left out."[4] The King yielded. May Tennant, first woman to serve as an Inspector of Factories, joined Lady Frances Balfour, though apparently with some reluctance.[5] Both were headlined in the press as the hearings commenced:

"Women as Judges of the Laws: The Commission on Divorce" (*The Illustrated London News,* March 12, 1910; see Illustration 4). The Church of England was represented by the Archbishop of York and Sir Lewis T. Dibdin. Considering the issues from the perspective of the working class and the poor were Mr. Thomas Burt, Mr. Edgar Brierley, and again May Tennant. Experts on legal matters were Lord Guthrie, Sir W. R. Anson, Judge Henry Tindal Atkinson, Sir Rufas Isaacs, and Brierley. The press would be represented by Mr. J. A. Spender, and the two houses of Parliament by Lord Derby and Sir George White. During its three-year tenure, the commission saw few changes: Sir Isaacs resigned relatively early to become Solicitor General and was replaced by Sir Frederick Treves, who brought medical expertise to the group. Lord Derby resigned late in the hearings and was not replaced; Sir George White died just as the final reports were being written.

How to characterize these commissioners, these arbitrators in the contest between England's stock stories and counterstories on divorce? Rebecca West gives us one way, seeing them in her fiery feminist youth as an unpromising assembly of people, impervious to ideas. The power of the Edwardian women's movement so overwhelmed them that they unwittingly ended up writing a feminist report. Chalk one up for Christabel Pankhurst.[6] Informed or deluded by years of friendship and work with many on the commission, the older feminist Balfour wrote more admiringly of her colleagues and their spirited deliberations, citing, in particular, exchanges with her old friends Lord Guthrie and J. A. Spender (Balfour 424).[7] To a columnist writing for *The Saturday Review,* the majority of the commissioners

WOMEN AS JUDGES OF THE LAWS: THE COMMISSION ON DIVORCE.

Drawing by S. Begg, our Special Artist, at the Commission; Faces Photographed by Elliott and Fry; Two by Lafayette.

CONSIDERING THE DIVORCES OF THE RICH AND OF THE POOR: THE ROYAL COMMISSION SITTING AT WINCHESTER HOUSE; AND PORTRAITS OF THE MEMBERS OF THE COMMISSION.

were radical extremists, sympathetic with those who were out to destroy the Christian ideal of marriage.[8] A characterization that lets us examine more neutrally the commissioners' actual activities as listeners within this arena is offered by Emery M. Roe in his analysis of the tangency of narrative and policy analysis. Whatever else they were, it seems fair to see the commissioners as a group of policy analysts confronted with "an issue of high uncertainty."[9] In his charge to the commission, King Edward saw the inquiry as examining two topics: the position of the poorer classes and England's publicity practices. The commissioners added to those topics, eventually organizing their inquiry under eight issues, which in turn reflect five questions (see Appendix I): Should the poor have access to the divorce court? Should procedures and regulations respecting separation orders be revised? Should grounds be made equal between men and women? Should the grounds be broadened? Should the present manner of publicizing divorce cases be modified?

Like policy analysts today, the commissioners studied these questions through lenses provided by tables of data, logical arguments with premises and conclusions, and a multiplicity of stories. Each lens has the potential to mislead, but on issues of high uncertainty, argues Roe, it is often the stories that present the greatest challenge. From them comes a "dual uncertainty" (559). First, as witnesses attempt to simplify or make more complex the issue under debate, they tell stories whose "truth value" cannot be ascertained. Second, "these dif-

OPPOSITE: 4 *The Appointment of Women Commissioners* (Illustrated London News, *March 12, 1910: 386*).

fering stories are often times conflicting, if not orthogonal to one another" (559). Should a policy analyst therefore disallow these unverifiable and contradictory
stories? Not at all. Like other advocates of narrative and
narrative analysis within the social sciences, Roe argues
that it is often the individual tale, the particular story,
that sheds light on a formerly invisible aspect of the issue, that offers startling insight into the human motives,
emotions, and ethical dilemmas inherent in a complex
policy problem. Certainly the commissioners felt the
need to hear stories. Witnesses will often begin a narrative, hesitate, ask if she or he should go on, and be urged
to continue. Who were the witnesses?

Between February 25, 1910, and the submission of its
final report in December 1912, the commission held
seventy-one sittings, taking evidence in fifty-six. Contacted through word of mouth and open invitations issued through the press, 246 witnesses came from all
over England bringing with them a range of interests,
perspectives, and narratives. The largest percentage
came from the law. Participants ranged from judges of
the High Court (the Right Honorable Sir John Bigham
and the Honorable Mr. Justice Bargrave Deane) to police court magistrates (including the well-known A. C.
Plowden and Cecil Chapman) to police court missionaries and rescue workers (among them Thomas Holmes,
frequent contributor to mainstream journals such as
Contemporary Review, but also the more obscure Miss
J. M. Tooke, Miss B. Leppington, Miss G. J. Morton, and
Miss E. Lidgett). Drawn again from the eminent and
the obscure, theologians and medical professionals
make up the next two largest groups. They are followed
in size of representation by members of the press; witnesses from associations (for example, the Associated

Societies for the Protection of Women and Children, the Mothers' Union of the Anglican Church, the Women's Cooperative Guild, the Women's Industrial Council, the Fabian Society, the Poor Man's Lawyer Department of the Cambridge University Settlement, etc.); and "miscellaneous witnesses" (Fru Ella Anker of Norway, well-known suffrage leader Millicent Garrett Fawcett, novelist Maurice Hewlett, and others). Another kind of testifying occurred through formal resolutions sent in by citizens' groups and through the approximately 350 letters received by the commission, many of them barely literate, all of them wishing to bring their own unsettling story to the commissioners' attention. [10]

As was true of the appointment of women to the commission, the soliciting of women as witnesses was seen as an important break with tradition. In her testimony, Margaret Llewelyn Davies speaks of the obstacles women had confronted when trying to express their views to the 1850 Commission on Divorce as well as to more recent parliamentary committees meeting on issues of concern to women. She repeats the astonishing comment made by the Home Secretary, Mr. Matthews, at a hearing on the Factory Bill of 1895. Said Mr. Matthews, "I have my own opinion as to what are the wishes of working women and to that opinion I shall always adhere" (*Report of the Royal Commission* 3:161). Though only 10 percent of the total, the female witnesses to the commission of 1912 were practicing doctors, political activists, workers within the local courts, and/or heads of large organizations or interest groups. Their words received coverage in the press and were frequently repeated within the commissioners' recommendations.

Some witnesses, it must be said, enter this arena with

no stories at all. They support their stance for or against alterations in the law with data and argument. The first two witnesses to appear, for example, are Lord Gorell's son, Henry Gorell Barnes, with comparative data on the laws of divorce in foreign countries, and Mr. A. Musgrave, one of the registrars for the High Court, with data on the costs of an Edwardian divorce. Similarly, the theologians who testify typically take the commissioners through detailed historical analyses of Christian doctrine and/or explications of biblical text but offer few local narratives. Many of the witnesses from the higher courts analyze and try to predict the effect that a change of venue—from the exclusive High Court in London to county or municipal courts—would have on both the rates of divorce and the daily working of England's court systems. And finally, support or criticism of the press is generally couched in the form of proposals for or against change rather than local narratives. (As Chapter 3 indicates, narratives that highlight the scandalous character of Edwardian publicity are a more salient feature of the novel.)

Far more likely to come into this arena with dramatic, evidentiary stories were doctors with a working-class clientele; witnesses who represented female interest groups; letter writers; and professionals from the lower courts, for example, police court magistrates, court missionaries, probation officers, and lawyers who contributed time to advising the poor. To ask why is to think again of Delgado's observation that counterstories tend to come from members of outgroups, or as is often the case here, from their representatives.

In the view of many who testified, it was women and the working class who were positioned as outsiders by the dominant narrative on divorce. A legal procedure existed to address marital failure, but it was extremely costly. Adultery was seen as the single necessary indicator of marital failure, but for wives, adultery alone was not a sufficient ground. In addition, neither women nor the working classes were likely to meet with anything like a peer if they did manage to bring a case to court. Witnesses wishing to rewrite the dominant narrative— be they themselves women or men, of the working class or not—approach the commissioners with a strategy. They will try, through counterstories, to create empathy for the suffering outsider and a vivid sense of the social disorder created by current policies. Through the well-told tale, they will try to shrink the distance between powerful listener (here, the policy analyst) and member of the outgroup.

As these poignant counterstories get told, advocates of the stock stories are incited to competition. The trading of tales is on. What I hope to show, as I trace one particular contest, is that in this arena the tellers of counterstories have a distinct advantage over their conservative competitors. I place Cecil Chapman at the beginning of this contest.

Trading Tales

A metropolitan magistrate from the Tower Bridge area of London with ten years' experience in dealing with separation orders, Chapman appears on May 25, 1910. As is typical of all who address a range of reforms rather than a single issue, Chapman offers a set of interrelated recommendations, supports them with narratives, and then is questioned by the commissioners.[11] Chapman would bring divorce trials into the local, metropolitan courts, encourage juries, and have women and men serving in equal numbers on the juries. He would create absolute equality of grounds between men and women and broaden the grounds so as to include cruelty, desertion, long penal sentences, incurable insanity, and alcoholism. He advocates limiting the kind of press coverage allowed. In thinking about how to strengthen marriage, he has two suggestions: He would make more visible its contractual obligations by insisting on a civil ceremony for everyone, with the religious ceremony optional, and he would make wives more economically independent through a legal right to a portion of their husband's wage. To him, a key problem in the conventional structuring of marriage and divorce was women's economic vulnerability. In emphasizing this, he launches a theme that will reverberate: In thinking of outsiders, no individual is more excluded from legal remedies than the wife who is poor.

How to convince the commissioners that his counterviews are credible? He tells stories, though wisely not only of suffering women. We hear, for example, of husbands married to incurably insane or alcoholic wives. We hear of abuses by certain local churches as they offer cut-rate marriage services, often to very young, poorly prepared candidates for marriage. But mostly we hear of destitute wives brutalized and humiliated by violent husbands. In arguing that the double standard regarding adultery undermines men's sense of morality, he offers this tale.

A wife came for a separation on account of the husband's cruelty, and the cruelty there relied upon was the fact that the husband had turned the wife out of his own bed and put her into the kitchen and taken another woman into his own bed. I asked, "How long has that occurred," and she said, "That has been going on for a long time; he has done that for the last month or so." I said, "It is perfectly monstrous that it should be so." I then said to the man, "What have you to say to that?" And the man said, "I have done nothing you can separate me for: after all, I have fed her, I have kept her, and given her a certain proportion of my wages; she has nothing to complain of because I prefer another woman." (*Report* 2:49)

End of story. Chapman moves on to his next point. What does the above tale do? With great economy, it gives a scene—wife banished to a bed in the kitchen, while off in the bedroom, husband cavorts with mistress, night after night, week after week.[12] It gives character: long-suffering wife finally turns to law; law turns to husband; husband thumbs nose at law. But equally important, distinguishing it from similar stories in the tabloids, this story lacks closure. It leaves the scandal uncontained, the disorder unresolved. The narrative energy that gets capped by the trial's awarding of a decree is left here pulsing. The effect is to shift attention to the listeners in this exchanging of narrative: You must do something to bring a proper closure to this unsettling tale.[13] Chapman is questioned at length about his various views—how would you institute this or that scheme, *where* are these so-called churches you speak of—and dismissed with thanks.

Over the months to come, his testimony will incite

responses critical and supportive. Among the most ada-
mant of his critics are the Honorable Mrs. Evelyn Hubbard and her colleague, Mrs. Emelini Steinthal, both
appearing five sessions later, on June 7, 1910. As vice-
president of the Mothers' Union, a Church of England
society, Mrs. Hubbard brought with her a petition bear-
ing 21,389 women's signatures. Confident that with
more time she could have gathered even more, she explains that the signers, all educated wives and mothers
who are opposed to liberalizing divorce, urge the commission not to extend any facilities or grounds for divorce, as such actions "would encourage the seeking of
divorce for trivial reasons" (*Report* 2:190).

Were it a practical suggestion, she would recommend
doing away with all divorce, in essence repealing the
Act of 1857. Realizing that such a reform is not likely,
she recommends keeping the law as it currently stands.
Chapman had argued that the concept of marriage as a
"sacred" act does not mean much to most people, even
those who are thoughtful and intelligent. Far more
comprehensible in his view is the sense of obligation
that comes from entering into an enforceable civil contract, such as one enters into with one's employer. Mrs.
Hubbard would agree with Chapman on the need to
increase a sense of obligation, but in her view marriage
simply *is* an expression of divine law. It is a sacred union
of man, woman, and God, a mystical reflection of
Christ's relationship to the Church. Announced in the
scriptures and interpreted by the Church of England
(Anglican Church), the law explicitly commands "that
the marriage vow lasts until death breaks it" (*Report*
2:191). One spouse may wrongfully break that vow,
but the other remains obliged to keep it.

Given her convictions, Hubbard finds herself in a dilemma. She would have rich and poor treated alike by the law, but she does not want to extend the effects of a law she believes to be morally wrong and socially harmful. If the general population fails to understand the sacredness of the vow, then surely the solution is to raise their religious understanding. To Chapman's sense that marital hardships and tragedies create national disorder—promiscuity, female poverty, domestic violence, unhealthy children—Mrs. Hubbard argues that "hardships and tragedies are to be borne . . . our view is that it is more likely to strengthen the national character and be for the advantage of the community for [people] to bear the hardships bravely than to legislate down to them" (*Report* 2:192). She is fully aware that hard cases occur, but maintaining an ideal—putting duty, responsibility, and self-sacrifice before happiness—is in the long run better for the nation as a whole. And the poor agree with her. Poor women especially do not want anything to do with divorce. They resent the idea, feeling "it will be for the advantage of the immoral and vicious" (*Report* 2:191).

Repeatedly asked by the commissioners, and by Lady Frances Balfour in particular, to support her views, Mrs. Hubbard defers to her colleague, appearing next. It is Mrs. Steinthal who has the evidence, the cases. In spite of the Archbishop of York's attempts to help Mrs. Hubbard restate her views in a more convincing manner, most of the commissioners are highly skeptical of her testimony. They criticize the wording of the petition she has brought in, the value of the signatures obtained (Anglican women who would not support such a protest had no way to record their views), and her

knowledge of working-class women.[14] Clearly her difficulties come partly from a sanctimonious tone, but they
also come from her paucity of tales. How can she speak
for others and yet bring in no tales that suggest an
awareness of their lives? We can attribute her weak performance to bad strategy on the part of her and Mrs.
Steinthal. But her basic philosophical stance also draws
her away from the personal, local narrative. People's individual lives in this vale of tears are finally not very
important, not when compared to eternal values and national ideals. The very goal of creating empathy for suffering spouses goes against her wish to take the long
view.

Arguing from much the same basic stance as Mrs.
Hubbard, Mrs. Steinthal fares better, though more I
suspect for her data and "pleasant, kind manner" than
for the quality of the stories she ends up submitting (*Report* 2:205). In meetings with mothers of the respectable
working class, the officials of the Mothers' Union have
gathered 85,491 votes to support a resolution to "protest
against any extension of the facilities or grounds for obtaining divorce" (*Report* 2:196). This vote, which is distinct from the more upper-class protests brought in by
Mrs. Hubbard, Mrs. Steinthal has come to deliver,
along with two books of evidence recording the views
of the officials of the Union. (See Appendix II.) Among
the twelve questions guiding the inquiry are the following: "Is there . . . a widespread or any demand for
greater facilities for divorce amongst the poor?" "If the
grounds of divorce were added to . . . would it tend to
lessen the sense of the binding character of the marriage
tie amongst the poor?" "Have you had personal experience in the working of separation orders granted by

magistrates? If so, what is your experience as to the frequency of subsequent reconciliation?" "Does the publication of newspaper reports of divorce cases . . . exercise a corrupting influence?" The commissioners carefully take Steinthal through all twelve questions and the approximately forty responses recorded for each. Not surprisingly, the officials indicate that there is no demand for divorce among the poor; that adding grounds would lessen the sense of the binding nature of the tie; that separations often lead to successful reconciliations; that separations also however lead to misconduct; and that the publication of newspaper reports exercises a corrupting influence. Within this set of views, Steinthal seems especially concerned to emphasize the lack of demand for divorce. Like Hubbard, she claims that working-class women resent divorce "being brought to their doors." They do not want it. She repeats an idea introduced by Hubbard. Upstanding working-class women feel that liberalizing divorce will reward the guilty. When Lord Gorell asks if these upstanding women would prefer that their guilty sisters "remain in a vicious state" rather than be helped out of it, she repeats that respectable women do not want to see vice made legal (*Report* 2:196).

Steinthal's books of evidence matter to the commissioners, getting them closer, it would seem, to the views of the working class, and especially working-class women. They spend a good deal of time taking her through her data. As they do so, it becomes clear that a key problem for those who support the reigning narrative is an appearance of indifference to the suffering of those to whom the current divorce law denies relief. How to avoid that appearance? Steinthal recommends more and better separations. A separation not only provides immediate relief, but it has the crucial advantage of keeping the sacred tie intact, allowing reconciliations and disallowing the adultery represented by a second marriage. Steinthal's stories, then, try to capture the many happy instances of reconciliation that occur. But such telling is not easy.

> 1. A man sent to prison for five years for attempting his wife's life, when he came out she received him back and has brought him to live a right life.
> 5. A couple separated for six months for the man's fault, wife determined to be patient and say nothing, all came right. He is now a splendid husband.
> 8. Separation which lasted from Friday to Sunday, happy making up.
> 10. A couple separated through fault on the man's side. He developed pneumonia, the wife went back to him, and they wished for a re-union, but the man died. (*Report* 2:205)

Steinthal has fourteen tales in all. A few are slightly more developed than the above, but none is as memorable as, for example, this counterstory of a forced reconciliation offered in rebuttal by Dr. Ethel Bentham.

> It has been urged that because in many cases of separation the parties afterwards return to one another, divorce is not necessary. But this is not a safe deduction. Many of these returns are for purely economic reasons. A woman applied for a separation order because of cruelty and unfaithfulness. Her husband had communicated venereal disease to her. She obtained her order and 8 shillings a week. The man went to prison rather than pay. She was unable to

earn, and eventually he forced her to return to him. She
had of course the alternatives of the workhouse or pros-
titution, and frankly discussed both with me. I happened
to be in medical charge of the case. She did try the workhouse, I suppose more or less on my advice, but she came
out saying that she had nothing in this world but her children, and she could not be separated from them. She did
return when the man came out of prison, after a long experience of the impossibility of getting any maintenance. She
returned to him, and he said he meant to pay her out for it
all, and he did. She lived a terrible life, and there were
other children, some born dead, two who have little
chance of being useful citizens. Many cases of the same sort
could be given. (*Report* 3:32)

A. C. Plowden generalizes the point.

The woman who gets [a separation] has to contrast her life
with what it was before she got it, and the effect of the
black eyes wearing off and the trial of life telling hard.
With small alimony and children, she may say, "It is six of
one and half a dozen of the other; if I go back I shall get
more black eyes, if not, I starve. I will risk it and go back."
But it does not follow that it is a permanent reconciliation.
She goes back, but how long does it last? . . . . She is
between the devil and the deep sea. (*Report* 2:274)

The commissioners wished to be impartial. They solicited stories that opposed as well as supported divorce.
But clearly a very brief story with a happy ending pales
beside a developed tale that leaves its characters longing
for release or content with their squalor and scandal.

I close my presentation of this one narrative exchange
with the testimony of A. C. Plowden and Margaret

Llewelyn Davies. Plowden's value here lies less in the local counterstories he told and more in the pungent way he challenged the dominant narrative. Though far from the last witness to appear, Davies brings to culmination many of the themes raised by Chapman, Hubbard, Steinthal, and Plowden. And she does so with data, argument, and 131 narratives.

Plowden appears on June 14, 1910, one week after Hubbard and Steinthal. Like Chapman, Plowden had been a metropolitan police court magistrate in London for twenty years. His colorful style of speech is arresting.[15] What does he think of the canonical narrative? That it is unreasonable and unjust, causing great suffering especially to women. Aspects of it, such as the Anglican vows, are positively obscene.

Agreeing with Chapman, he sees marriage as a civil contract, much like a partnership. But he does not think Chapman goes far enough. In his view, divorce is absolutely necessary to marriage. Without the possibility of divorce, acting as an insurance policy, marriage would be a "dangerous, mad gamble" (*Report* 2:271). There is an unreasoning prejudice against divorce that comes from the mistaken linkage of marriage and mystical matters, from taking the "ultra spiritual view" (*Report* 2:276).

In fact, if judicial separation may be considered something of a medicine that secures instant but temporary relief, divorce is like a surgical procedure. By granting the parties real independence from each other and the chance to remarry, divorce brings a genuine and lasting cure. The "disease" is any breach of the contract, with "breach" defined by whatever grounds "receive the assent of the large, intelligent, and sensible portion of the community" (*Report* 2:272). He himself would include infidelity, desertion, cruelty, and bigamy as absolute causes. More questionable for him are grounds related to penal sentences and lunacy. He is strongly in favor of divorce for incompatibility of temper, which opens the door, he realizes, for divorce by mutual consent. "By our law as it stands," he asserts, "two people are not allowed to ask for a recision of this contract; one is—it must be one—and that one is supposed to ask for it reluctantly with a certain degree of coyness, and with its hands before its face. The law grants it blushing" (*Report* 2:272).

As for male/female inequity on the ground of adultery, he would leave any revisions entirely to women. He believes that most women take a more severe stance on the infidelities of other women than on the infidelities of men; thus they may very well agree with the assumptions on which the current law rests. Pressed on that perception by Lady Frances Balfour and Lord Gorell, he repeats his fundamental stance: "I think the law has dealt so inconsiderately with women in all legislation affecting the relations between the sexes that I should be very loth to see any grievance which a woman suggests as a grievance not be addressed" (*Report* 2:272).

Focusing on legal procedures, Plowden joins Chapman in believing that municipal courts are the appropriate venue for divorce trials. He would, however, institute certain changes. Referring to bastardy cases, he exclaims, "It is a cruel and humiliating thing which makes a young woman come into court crowded with men and go step by step through every feature, phase, and detail of her betrayal and fall, and then be cross examined on the top of that by a not too scrupulous advocate" (*Report* 2:274). Given his whole approach to marriage and divorce, the only question is "whether the benefits of divorce—I go so far as to call them blessings—should not be extended to the poorer classes" (*Report* 2:271).

Plowden is roundly attacked by one commissioner or another during the questioning period. Occasionally he modifies his views. For example, he expresses reservations about incompatibility as a ground for divorce when confronted with the possibility of divorces being granted if only one spouse is unhappy, and he softens his comment regarding the obscenity of the Anglican marriage service. But on his two major points he stands firm. First, in altering those aspects of the divorce laws that currently foster gender inequity, he would give women the power to decide the changes. Second, the reigning narrative's view of divorce as shameful is foolish and wrong. "Divorce consolidates and strengthens the marriage tie if it is properly understood. . . . Rightly or wrongly, I never sleep so soundly after a day's work as when I feel I have separated some woman from a brute of a husband on grounds which are unanswerable . . . and I should rejoice more if . . . I could give what is at that moment her heart's desire, and what she deserves by the law of the land, a divorce" (*Report* 2:273).

Plowden's testimony comes near the end of the spring 1910 hearings. After eight more sessions, the commission adjourns for a summer recess, starting up again in late October. The break, it appears, was fortunate for Margaret Llewelyn Davies. Able to analyze the performance of Hubbard and Steinthal and the commissioners' apparent receptivity to Plowden's views on female self-determination, Davies had time to carry out a more thorough survey of working-class women's views than could Steinthal and to gather together a rich array of stories to dramatize the survey's findings.[16]

Appearing on November 9, 1910, Davies came as general secretary of the Women's Cooperative Guild. Established in 1883, the guild was a working-class women's organization, operating as a part of the Co-operative Union, Ltd., itself a labor organization designed to strengthen the consumer power of working-class families. Throughout England and Wales, 520 branches of the guild were active, with 25,897 women participating. In contrast to the Mothers' Union, whose local officials were generally "ladies" while the members were working class, the membership of the guild, local officers and members alike, were all working class. They were not of "the lowest class," Davies readily admits, but absolutely of the working class—and in a position to know intimately the lives of the truly poor.

Through the guild, Davies had conducted two surveys. (See Appendix II.)[17] She had sent two questions to 431 branches, representing 23,501 members: 1) "Do you think the grounds for divorce should be the same for men as for women, as they now are in Scotland?" and 2) "Do you think divorce proceedings should be cheapened, so that divorce may be within reach of the poor?" The branches had voted at their meetings and sent in their responses. A more detailed survey, consisting of the above two questions and five more, had been sent out to 124 local officials of the guild, selected "on account of their intelligence . . . and with no regard to their views on the subject, which were unknown in every case" (*Report* 3:149). Thus, Davies implies, in contrast to the surveys conducted by the Mothers' Union, the guild's surveys would genuinely present the views of working-class women—by far the largest group of women in the nation—and were not biased by a preselection strategy. In keeping with the guild's general goal of empowering working-class women to articulate their own views on public issues, Davies's method of delivery is to introduce a survey question, enumerate the responses, and then read a series of direct quotations, in the form of "cases" and "opinions," from the respondents.

Davies prefaces her presentation with several points. First, she calls attention to the intensity of interest the commission's hearings and the guild's survey have inspired. She greatly regrets that the commissioners cannot see the actual letters sent in by guild women, "often many pages long, laboriously written after thought and consultations" (*Report* 3:149). She then quotes from such branch comments as "caused the best discussion we have ever had" (*Report* 3:150). Second, she wants the commission to understand that while the results of the surveys show a clear consensus, the women of the guild do not speak with one voice. She scrupulously quotes from members with religious objections to all divorce and from one branch secretary who writes cogently against liberalizing divorce out of concern for female poverty: "For if the poor get divorce easy, and there are 4 or 5 children, who will keep the wife and children, as we know the woman would not be able to support them: then they fall on the State" (*Report* 3:150). And third, Davies gives an overview of certain principles she sees guild women expressing in their responses to the survey. It is clear that they feel a bad marriage is much harder on a woman than on a man. Chances are she will be suffering emotionally, financially, and physically.

Further, speaking directly to the religious stance taken by the Mothers' Union, Davies argues that most guild women see the sacredness of the tie as dependent entirely on there being love and respect between wife and husband. Where such does not exist, there is no sacred bond. Hindering both the maintaining of a good marriage and the possibility of a divorce where necessary are traditional perceptions of the wife as the property of the husband; married women's economic dependency, especially where there are children; the fact that children are still seen as the father's property; and the dread of public disgrace. She develops each of these latter four issues in turn, reading from the guild women's letters.

Moving on to the survey, she interrupts herself with "Shall I continue with all this?" "Yes," responds Lord Gorell, "I think this is so valuable, we ought to have it all" (*Report* 3:152). A pattern is established, with her reading the question, giving a breakdown of the responses, and then supporting those responses with a series of stories, followed by opinions. Her reading of Question 2b is typical. "Should all costs of Divorce proceedings be paid by the State where necessary? Individual replies: Ninety-seven women out of 124 reply in the affirmative, of whom, six are opposed to or doubtful about divorce. Six women reply in the negative of whom three are opposed to or doubtful about divorce. Four are doubtful. Seventeen do not reply" (*Report* 3:153). Several supporting stories follow, including this one.

A woman wished to obtain a divorce, but had to wait till after the birth of her baby. Her husband left her alone in London, a few weeks before the birth of her child. She knew no one, she had no money, and he had pawned all her jewelry. When the baby was born the doctor wished to send for her father as she was in such a terrible condition. When she was strong enough she went with the baby to her people in Manchester. With the help of her father, she managed to obtain enough money to start proceedings, and the case was dated for some time before the long vacation. She had to come with her baby from Manchester to London, find lodgings for herself, then find her witnesses, one of whom was the nurse, who had to be paid, as she lost her employment for the time she appeared. The doctor, in spite of his action at the child's birth, refused to appear as a witness. After being in London several days, some of which were spent entirely in the Law Courts, she was told that, owing to other cases, the divorce case could not be heard until after the vacation. Owing to the need for money, she was unable to proceed any further. (*Report* 3:153)

Opinions include: "It is much harder for poor people to live together, if either party are wanting a divorce, as they cannot get away from each other as rich people can." "A question of justice should not depend on monetary power." (*Report* 3:154)

In these opinions, by the way, one often reads comments on, even paraphrases of, the testimony of earlier witnesses to the commission as reported through the newspapers. There is a genuine national conversation going on here, and working-class women are participating.

In all, Davies brings to the commission a grand total of 131 stories, fifty-seven of which she reads aloud in giving her proof, with the remaining seventy-four published as an appendix to her testimony. Within the latter is a category titled "Personal Stories" including four very long, first-person accounts. The following is representative.

At the age of 25, I married a man of my own station, one that I believed would make me a suitable helpmate, but a very short time after marriage I was forced to realize intoxicating drink had for him a far greater fascination than home or wife. . . . [Davies's ellipsis] One evening, hoping to keep him from bad company, I went to the warehouse at which he was engaged and met him after work hours. In the presence of his shop mates he drew me to him, kissed me, saying how pleased he was I came, but directly we were alone he cursed me for trying to spoil his pleasure, and all the way home threatened what he would do when we got there. I was not accustomed to talk to my neighbors. Shame held me silent. This he knew. When we reached home, he pushed me in the passage and locked the door. Then to terrify me he beat a chair into small pieces against the wall, and also threw the burning lamp to the ground; and when I tried to extinguish the blaze, he threw me also to the floor and held me there, until the floor cloth became alight. [Paragraphs follow as the woman writes of separation orders, attempts at reconciliation, her husband's continually telling people that she is not really his wife, and her eventual decision to disappear into a factory job.] . . . . During the last 15 years I have lived working and supporting myself. I might have filled a better position than just a factory hand, as I am today, had I not always been in dread of my vagabond husband appearing on the scene as he had frequently done, covering me with humiliation and shame and spreading the vilest rumors about me reflecting on my character; but the fact that I have been in one employ the whole time should, I think, speak for my character. I am personally looking forward with hope that divorce will be

brought within reach of the people, and I shall be one of
the first to try for that relief, not because I hope or wish to
remarry, but because I cordially long to regain that freedom which will relieve me from the necessity of passing
myself off as a widow. Case 114, from Yorkshire (*Report*
3:167)

Constructing a counterstory, this woman from Yorkshire employs two consistent strategies: She confronts
the assumptions of the stock story head-on, and she
quotes the language of the stock story in order to re-
shape it for her own ends. The reigning narrative advises suffering people to take the long view. She forces
the listener to attend to the short view—the smashed
chair, the burning rug, her body forced and held to the
floor.[18] This up-close description of abuse is then repeated as she recounts years of suffering. Further, she
resituates the site of humiliation. Shame does not reside
in the acquiring of a divorce but in her husband's lies
about their relationship and in the subterfuges she has
had to practice. It is not as an accepting and forgiving
wife that she claims "character," but as a single individual and responsible employee. The "freedom" she desires is not the license to remarry, but the freedom to tell
the painful but respectable truth about herself. Like so
many other storytellers in this arena, she ends by turning to her listeners, asking for empathy and action.

Throughout, in both substance and mode of presentation, Davies's evidence challenges that of Hubbard
and Steinthal. Her data present directly contrary findings, most important, that working-class women desire
reform and believe that divorce should be seen as a potential social good, at times even a duty. In addition, her

data raise issues and construct images unimagined by her conservative sisters. Hubbard and Steinthal envision married women, positioned inside their homes, passively peering out at the threat of divorce "being brought to their doors." Davies and her survey invite women to see themselves as actively involved in shaping and administering the law. "Should women serve on juries?" asks Question 7b. Four women say no, 104 say yes, three are doubtful, and thirteen do not reply. In support comes story fifty-five.

> I would like to say to you that I had the painful duty of being at the inquest on a girl—just went with the mother. The girl was in trouble and so drowned herself, and I was horrified at that inquest to see how lightly the case was taken up with regard to the girl, and no word of warning to the lad nor chastised in any way, and I say Yes from my heart from only that one inquest I see the need for women to be on juries or anything where women are concerned. (*Report* 3:160)

The subsequent opinions argue for women serving on juries considering any issue, as well as becoming professionals throughout the legal system.

In the closing portion of her proof, "A Point of View," Davies elaborates on a concern that is often raised in the hearings and has risen to prominence over this century, that is, the causal relationship between female poverty and divorce. As Mr. Spender puts it, case after case within Davies's testimony has argued for the need to liberalize divorce laws in response to the sufferings of women. But case after case has also demonstrated that much of the suffering of women is caused by economic disadvantages. If rising rates of divorce would lead to an increase in female poverty, asks Spender, should one not hesitate to recommend easier divorce? No, responds Davies. "The economic question will have to be dealt with, but our attitude toward divorce cannot depend on it." Her sense of the women's view is "they wish to have an opportunity of being free, and would risk the economic difficulties" (*Report* 3:169).

In tracking this one narrative exchange, I have sought to give the reader a sense of how stories were used by witnesses to the Royal Commission. Narratives in general entered the hearings as a way to bolster an argument and put flesh on statistics. Counterstories, designed to resist the stock stories and create empathy with English women and men ill served by the current law, clearly pulled ahead in the competition. Far better than could the stock stories, they dramatized sufferings, longings, frustrations, inequities. Which issues were emphasized by the counterstories told in this arena? Which were slighted?

The counterstories offered to the Royal Commission tended to resist the reigning narrative's position on a range of concerns. Counterstories refuted the mystical nature of the marriage vow; the advantages of separations over divorces; the social value of a gendered division of labor; the differing significance of male and female adultery; the centrality of adultery as an indication of marital failure; the danger of allowing the working class access to divorce; the fairness of a legal system run entirely by men.

In opposing these stands, the counterstories urged a definition of marriage that emphasized the kinds of obligations a civil contract places on two responsible adults.

They dramatized the suffering and disorder caused by permanent separations and the female poverty caused by the current division of labor. Addressing male adultery, the counterstories sought to capture the horrors of venereal disease, often brought home from a casual encounter, for infected wives and children. In expanding the ways one can conceive of marital failure beyond the act of adultery, they proffered image after image of wife battering, child abuse, failure to maintain, alcoholism, and insanity. As for the working class and its morals, the counterstories praised English workers for their basic decency and/or painted pictures of the squalor in which many lived owing to England's bad laws. In Davies's testimony, the counterstories gave the working class a voice in the proceedings. The possibility of a change in legal processes, so as to include women, drew forth stories that emphasized both the desire of women to participate and the impoverishment of understanding that was occurring through the exclusion of women. No one was sure that adding women to the legal system would make the law more sympathetic to women plaintiffs, but the need for women to be incorporated into the judicial process was clearly argued.

In general, these counterstories were confronting the stock stories' definition of disorder, especially as disorder was imagined within a working-class context. The stock story saw the unattached adult, male or female, as restless, dangerous, diseased, and irresponsible. The law must maintain the kinds of bonds that constrain this person's mobility, that prevent him or her from breaking up a home and going out on the streets. The counterstories located danger, disease, and disorder *inside* the failed marriage and confining home. As was envisioned by aspects of Lloyd George's welfare agenda, the law needed to enter into English homes and improve conditions. Here, with respect to divorce law reform, the law must find a way to release a trapped spouse. To allow this spouse to leave the mate who is abusive, alcoholic, insane, or in the case of a husband, unwilling to fulfill his economic responsibilities, is to provide a remedy for chaos, disorder, and disease.

What kinds of counterstories do *not* get told during the hearings? First, very few of the counterstories are able to imagine life after divorce in any detail, apart from the possibility of remarriage. Few, for example, create narratives that are able to dramatize the often mentioned issue of increasing rates of female poverty. Alternatively, few helped the commissioners imagine the divorced person as an individual figure of productivity or growth.

Second, perhaps because the hearings were an official, state-sponsored ceremony, almost no one takes the libertarian stance that the state has no business in people's private affairs, one way or another. Few voices in this arena turned on the state, calling it a voyeur in its very staging of divorce trials, a snoop when it inquired into marriage. The focus of these counterstories is on extending the scope of the state's power to people not receiving its benefits.

Finally, few counterstories focus on children. Mention is made of children suffering through the current restrictive laws, and of course, stock stories responded with predictions of the ways children would suffer through increased rates of divorce. But as Eekelaar writes, the welfare of children was not part of the "official problem" the commission had set itself.[19] In the Edwardian divorce trial and in these hearings, children remained an "ancillary" issue. Each of the above concerns becomes a major focus in the novel. I close with an evaluation of the storytelling that went on in this arena from the perspectives of the storytellers and listeners.

Que Vaut le Récit?

In selecting the narrative exchange between Chapman, Hubbard, Steinthal, Plowden, and Davies, I highlighted as something new and noteworthy the presence of women's voices in this public conversation. Let me try to analyze here what the woman storytellers got out of participating in the hearings. Did it make any real difference that they were finally being included in a debate over divorce?

One can easily speculate that the commission would have reached the same recommendations had no women testified and/or that the voices of Hubbard, Steinthal, Davies, and Bentham canceled each other out. But there are better ways to measure the difference it made for Edwardian women to have testified before the Royal Commission.

An affirmative analysis emphasizes the value of women joining legal systems and legislative deliberations, whether as professionals, witnesses, letter writers, or whatever, by focusing less on predetermined outcomes and more on social processes. As Kirp, Yudof, and Franks argue, the damage done to women by a patriarchal legal system may lie less in the particular laws that system may enact—though particular laws can clearly disadvantage women—

and more in its usurpation of women's decision-making powers.[20] Be the woman the Honorable Evelyn Hubbard, Dr. Ethel Bentham, Margaret Llewelyn Davies, Miss J. M. Tooke, or the writer from Yorkshire, to grant her a role in the formation of public policy is to see her as a citizen with experiences, a point of view, and a voice. Hubbard and her conservative colleagues came to the commission with a dearth of effective stories, but they very much needed to be there, for their own sake, the sake of the women they represented, and the education of the commissioners and public. Kirp, Yudof, and Franks do not speak to a further value—that of networking—but it shows up very clearly in the testimony of Davies, Bentham, Steinthal, and others.[21] As Edwardian women constructed and shared knowledge with each other, over divorce, the vote, a minimum wage, they built consensus, clarified disagreement, and strengthened their sense of themselves as members of interest groups and as individual citizens.

And what about the vast numbers of women who did not come in person to the hearings but handed off their tales to their respective representatives? How well did this process serve them? The easy story here, I believe, would measure the loss involved in the very fact that they, working-class women especially, were only "represented." W.J.T. Mitchell is right when he quips there is no representation without taxation.[22] An inevitable loss occurs whenever one person's experience is translated into a representation by another. Would it not have been preferable for the woman from Yorkshire, for example, to have come up to London and spoken in her own behalf? Perhaps. But the arguments developed by Bottomley and Massaro, discussed in Chapter 1, urge us to question this assumption. In comparing the way formal and informal adjudication processes work for the less powerful party, Bottomley urges us to recognize the advantages that adhere to formal trials. Among them is the right to be represented by a professional who is trained to mitigate the power imbalances that exist in the culture at large.[23] By implication, her argument urges us to see the process followed by the Royal Commission's formal hearings as similarly advantageous to the less powerful. A witness like Davies, taking on the role of advocate, delivered working-class women's tales in a form the commissioners could recognize and in a context that gave the tales cumulative weight. In certain respects, she took on the task that Elizabeth Schneider sees as central to the work of the lawyer who represents lesbians, gays, and feminists in the courtroom: "We translate that which we do not think someone else [the judge or jury] will understand."[24]

Davies not only "translated" and conveyed working-class women's views in a highly effective manner, she and her colleagues, male and female, delivered a sophisticated critique of the ways the canonical tale muffled women and men of all classes. First, she urged legal recognition of more—and more complex—plots on marital failure. Second, she insisted that the price of admission into the courtroom be lowered. Third, perceiving that the price is not only financial, she argued that public disgrace is often the wrong response to the person who seeks a divorce. If it is shame that keeps many people silent, then the shaming should stop.

As Davies and others speak to the possibility of women administering the law, they bring up one further issue regarding the muffling of women. If a woman gets to court and tries to tell a counterstory, she may find that there is no one to hear her, no one to able to interpret her experience. Swanwick argues specifically against the standard Edwardian practice of clearing the courtroom of all women during the rehearsal of painful or explicit evidence. It is very much in the interest of the female plaintiff or defendant, she contends, that women listeners remain in the courtroom. They validate the female speaker (*Report* 2:461). As witnesses testify on the need for women to act as listeners—solicitors, barristers, judges, members of the jury, the assembled public—they are speaking directly to the crucial role interpretive communities play in the construction of meaning.[25]

In brief, I contend, the women storytellers in this arena gave and gained much by participating. So too I believe the commissioners accomplished a great deal, initially in their role as listeners and then as storytellers themselves. Lord Gorell had pinned his hopes on the commission being able to produce a unanimous set of recommendations. When it became clear at the January 30, 1912, meeting that there would definitely be a minority report, Gorell was very disappointed.[26] Although he continued to work hard on the report throughout 1912 and published the four-volume document in November of that year, Gorell was exhausted and died five months later in April 1913.[27] Other commissioners apparently felt a similar frustration. Markham writes of May Tennant, "like other signatories of the Majority Report, she had the consciousness of three years of labour largely wasted in discussions and antagonisms that were irreconcilable" (43). Both expressions of disappointment imply that because the listeners were not persuaded to a uniform position, the hearings had been a failure.

Others took a different view. Lord Gorell's son, Henry Gorell Barnes, who had served as secretary to the commission, was eager during 1913 and the first part of 1914 to emphasize the points on which the commissioners had agreed.[28] Unanimously they had supported lowering the cost of divorce by allowing local courts to exercise jurisdiction over divorce; they had agreed on establishing equity between the sexes; they were united on limiting publicity; and they agreed on specific recommendations related to separation orders and the declaring of nullity. The only real point of disagreement was on the proposal to extend grounds beyond adultery. Had not the war intervened, had he not been killed in France, one can imagine the younger Gorell Barnes campaigning for changes on the above points of agreement. In her own way, Rebecca West also emphasized the extent to which the commissioners had agreed, most importantly on their support for gender equity.

Roe would have us question both kinds of evaluation. On issues of high uncertainty, it may be foolish to circulate an appearance of unanimity while downplaying the unknowns and disagreements that continue to plague the community's understanding of the issue. At the same time, it may be equally inaccurate to disparage an analysis that contains within its conclusion obdurate disagreements. If policy analysts deliver a final report that heightens awareness and refines understanding of both unanimity and dissension, they may consider their efforts a success. Such a report can indicate a true evaluation of the tales that were told and needs to become part of what Roe calls the "metastory" toward which the policy analyst and legislator keep working.

What the commissioners offered Parliament was precisely the kind of report that could heighten awareness and refine understanding. They solicited and listened to the views of the people; they organized and recorded an extremely complex social conversation. They then responded with an analysis of the law that envisioned it as a very powerful way of imagining the real.

Unanimously the commissioners recommended legal changes that posited the following unorthodox views of reality. First, estranged working-class husbands and wives are moral and responsible adults who deserve access to divorce. Second, the physical and spiritual natures of women and men are sufficiently alike as to make it wrong for any law respecting divorce to treat them differently. And third, seeking a divorce should not be considered shameful, deserving of public humiliation and widespread publicity. Shared by conservatives and liberals, these are not insignificant revisions of how things are or should be.

Regarding the commissioners' disagreement, one observes that in recommending the extending of grounds, the majority asserted a new view of English marriage. Marriages, they claimed, are dissolved de facto by willful desertion, sustained cruelty, incurable insanity, imprisonment under a commuted death sentence, habitual drunkenness, and of course adultery. When a nation's law turns a blind eye to reality—the above reality regarding marriage or any other—the citizens of that nation will hold the law in contempt. This contempt leads to immorality. Marriage and morality in England will be improved if the grounds of divorce are broadened.

Posing an alternative view of reality, the minority argues that broadening the grounds for divorce historically leads to an increase in the rates of divorce. This increase will occur in England just as it has in all other

Western nations, and English citizens and institutions will thereby suffer. Seeing divorce as a way to address the very real problems of marriage is fallacious. If the community wishes to address the suffering of unhappy wives and husbands, it must direct its thinking to much earlier phases in the failing marriage. And because all three signers of the Minority Report identify with the Church of England, they envision marriage being improved by enhanced religious understanding. As with the views of reality unanimously shared by the commissioners, the views on which the commissioners disagreed are significant, with each side's perspective meriting attention.

It was in pursuit of Roe's latter goal—policy analysts working with legislators to construct an adequately complex metastory—that the rich process of telling and listening in this arena ceased. The liberal government accepted the commissioners' report but refused to listen to or discuss its findings. Time and again in 1913 and 1914, individual members of Parliament submitted bills or raised questions regarding the report. Time and again, Asquith avoided or deflected the issue. It was a lost opportunity. Appendix I indicates the piecemeal way in which the commission's recommendations got legislated, some sooner, some later, none logically linked to the others, nor to the minority's prescient concerns. In brief, Parliament failed to take advantage of the report's rich resources to design a coherent policy, one that would respond to the national conversation which the report so thoughtfully articulated.[29]

Stock Stories versus Counterstories: The Novel

May—th—The world is riotously beautiful—I am riotously happy—I should like to have the power to make every being on the face of the earth as happy as I am. . . . Today I had my *decree absolute*!!!
> —Alice M. Deihl, *The Confessions of Perpetua* (1912)

Whereas in our father's day . . . novels ended with marriage and happiness, now they more often commence with marriage and misery, and frequently end with divorce.
—Father Henry Day S.J., *Marriage, Divorce, and Morality* *(1912)*

In their separate accents, both of the above voices from 1912 bear witness to an Edwardian phenomenon: the novel of divorce. Issued sporadically early in the decade, by 1912 the divorce novel forms a clear subgenre within the fiction of the day.[1] I begin with background on these novels and then move to the central question of this chapter: How do the divorce novels reinforce, resist, or expand upon the narratives produced by the trials, tabloids, and hearings of the Royal Commission.

Mapping the Territory

Like any narrative, the Edwardian novel was intimately shaped by circumstance and convention. In particular, it reflected changes that had occurred in the production of novels during the 1890s. Compared to the Victorian novel—issued in three volumes, priced at thirty-one shillings, and often borrowed from a circulating library—the turn-of-the-century novel was considerably shorter, considerably cheaper.[2] Continuing this trend, the Edwardian novel typically consisted of one volume running approximately 300 to 350 pages. It was inexpensively bound in cloth, tended to lack the illustrations one sees liberally sprinkled throughout Victorian fiction, and cost a mere six shillings. It was clearly intended for purchase by individual readers. Advertisements for upcoming novels often follow upon the last pages of the story, puffs that warn readers not to miss this or that forthcoming novel. It promises to be "*the* outstanding success" of the season. Well distributed, novels could be bought at railway stations and a variety of shops throughout England, from H. H. Smith to the ubiquitous Boots. Borrowing from a private or municipal library also remained a popular option.

The advertisements posted in the end pages were derived from the astonishing number of reviews that Edwardian novels received. Arnold Bennett writes that a well-placed novel would often get as many as forty reviews and that its publishers would see that it got advertised in a daily paper for two or three months running, four or five days a week.[3] Many writers of popular fiction brought out at least a book a year, or expected under normal circumstances to do so (Bennett, *How to Become an Author* 23, 191–192). Those who turned out a divorce novel typically wrote on a range of topics, were well respected in their professions, and generally made a good to excellent living from their craft.[4] A solid success would sell approximately ten thousand copies. A bestseller—a "boom" book in Wells's words—could sell as many as 100,000 copies.[5] Clearly novels were big business. At the same time, if one thinks back to the sales figures given for the mass circulation Sunday tabloids, even Wells's best-seller pales by comparison: *News of the World* boasted weekly sales of 1 million copies, and the top four metropolitan Sunday papers added together claimed weekly sales of approximately 6.5 million.[6] Sales figures for either a novel or a newspaper do not of course tell the whole story respecting readership, given that both typically passed through more than one set of hands. Still, in asking what kinds of stories most Edwardians read when they read about divorce, we must envision even the most popular of the divorce novels attracting less than one-tenth of the readership drawn to tabloid taunting and sensationalism.

What kinds of readers did the novel seek? In contrast to the inexpensive, highly illustrated, and quickly read tabloids aimed largely at England's vast working class, Edwardian popular novels seem clearly designed for the middle class.[7] Reading them required significant leisure. The price of purchase, while moderate when compared to Victorian prices, was equivalent to a week's rent for a working-class family living in London.[8] Throughout, the language of even the more adventuresome novels is characterized by a tone of respectability, and the strategy employed in the closing advertisements implies an audience of competitive consumers. The cast of characters in the divorce novels is, in itself, predominantly middle to upper class. An occasional divorce novel focuses on the struggles of the working poor (the anonymously published *My Husband Still*,[9] May Sinclair's *The Combined Maze,* and Vincent Brown's *Mayfield,* for example), but most are interested in exploring ethical and psychological issues that become discussable only if the initial hurdle of cost is rendered moot.

The Edwardian novel seems also to have been aimed at men and women readers, at "the bored female and burdened male," says Hunter (52). Given the divorce novel's particular interest in legal reform, Claud Cockburn's characterization of the novel's audience as the nation's mandarin class—civil service officials, solicitors, members of Parliament, clergy, doctors, and solicitors—is significant.[10] If Edwardian novels did not reach the sheer quantity of readers attracted by the Sunday papers, they did reach readers with the potential to influence changes in national policy.

Though Father Day joined others in seeing the advent of the divorce novel as a very bad sign of the times, other Edwardians welcomed the kind of problem fiction it represented. Maud Braby, witty commentator on modern marriage and occasional novelist herself, constructed a brief history of the Edwardian novel in her *Modern Marriage and How to Bear It.* As she saw it, fiction writers of the 1880s and early 1890s had staged a rebellion against conservative treatments of marriage and sexuality. Problem novels, along with the short stories published in *The Yellow Book,* had courageously examined a series of delicate and difficult issues. But this brave impulse was squelched by mid-decade. (Braby does not refer to the chilling effect of the Oscar Wilde trial in 1895, but later historians have seen it as highly influential.) Thoughtful readers in the latter years of the century were forced to make do with escapist novels consisting of much plot and little analysis or psychology. But as the new century began to find its feet, a new set of problem novels emerged (*Modern Marriage* 6–8).

As did Ford Madox Ford, H. G. Wells, and E. M. Forster, Braby saw the new novels as exciting in their attempts to adopt some of the premises and techniques of French realism.[11] In Forster's words, these new novels demonstrated a commitment to writing honestly, pessimistically if need be, about everyday problems in English life ("Pessimism in Literature"). They showed a kind of "coming home" from the escapism of their immediate predecessors (Hunter 235).

When Edwardian writers interested specifically in divorce "came home" to the problem of marriage, however, they adopted a different approach from that taken by earlier novelists and from their own colleagues. As Ardis and Miller demonstrate, the traditional marriage plot of the eighteenth and nineteenth centuries was effectively discredited by the New Woman novels of the 1880s and 1890s.[12] Few serious novelists writing during the Edwardian decade felt they could solve their plot's complications with a traditional wedding (see Forster's "Pessimism in Literature" 135–136). Courtship was out; structured as a problem, marriage was in. As Miller suggests however, to denigrate old plots and exhausted structures is one thing; to write beyond them is something else.

In exciting ways, writes Miller, Edwardian marriage novels struggled against traditional cultural and narrative assumptions. But the results were uneven. Especially in the crucial moment of the novel's ending, the allure of a happy closure and reconstituted couple often won out. Do novels specifically about divorce distinguish themselves within this larger category of problematic marriage fictions? If we focus on endings, the differences are negligible. As in the marriage novels, some divorce novels write beyond the conventional;

many do not. Predictably, among those that do not are the conservative, anti-divorce novels. But novels do more than end.[13] For entire afternoons or evenings, they pull their readers into the woods of the narrative, offering unsettling images, unconventional motivations, new ways of seeing. Working with material not found in the other marriage novels, the divorce novels in general push the reader to wrestle in new ways with the tensions between the private and public faces of marriage; to recognize the conflicting desires of parents and children; and to complicate understanding of intergenerational sexual dynamics. Those that argue for liberalizing the law urge readers to broaden their vision of what constitutes a respectable home; to expand the imagery associated with separated people; and to entertain the notion that an adulterous wife just might be an admirable and plucky soul.[14]

Perhaps the most salient feature of the divorce novels is their refusal, as a group, to toe any one narrative line. A map of the territory reveals an extraordinary range of plots and stances. At the very outset, the novels can be sorted into ones that begin with a divorce and trace its effects, or begin with a happy marriage, dramatize a descent into misery, and conclude with a divorce, be it secured, foiled, or ultimately resisted.

Overlapping the above, one can distinguish between novels that argue for or against liberalizing the law. Those that seek to liberalize tend to dramatize the characters' sufferings in terms that correspond with the specific legal grounds under debate by witnesses to the Royal Commission, from alcoholism to insanity to incompatibility. The pro-reform novels then either deliver the unhappy spouse from the hell he or she is in, or slam the door to freedom in the character's desperate face. When they slam the door, these novels resemble many of the embedded narratives offered to the Royal Commission: If convinced, the reader goes away frustrated by the status quo and eager for change. Though many of the reform novels focus on the sufferings of a trapped wife, trapped husbands and couples occur as well. If the focus is on a couple, both husband and wife see the marriage as a wasteland and join in common cause to wrest freedom from the state. They may or may not succeed.

If specific grounds are not the target in a pro-reform novel, procedural matters may be. Several denounce the conventions of adversarial law, the overwhelming presence of the male gaze within the judiciary, the open court system, and England's publicity practices.

Countering the reform novels, the conservative novels typically adopt a religious perspective. They may reward their suffering spouses for ultimately turning back from a contemplated divorce; they may punish them for carrying it through; they may close with a deathbed repentance. Most draw upon the hard doctrine of *contemptus mundi*. Like conservative witnesses to the Royal Commission, they grant the earthly suffering and longings of unhappy spouses, but they maintain we are only pilgrims on this earth. The teaching of the New Testament is clear: Marriage is a sacrament between man, woman, and God. Representing high idealism and inexhaustible charity, the indissoluble contract of marriage symbolizes the forgiving love of Christ for his people, the aspiring love of the people for Christ. To allow one's marriage to be put asunder may release body, heart, and mind, but such an act will sully the soul. At their best, the conservative novels explicitly air what many of the reform novels mute: the ethical dilemmas of divorce; the pain of abandoning a once-loved mate; and the guilt, even the irrational guilt, that may follow upon the breaking of a vow in which one has believed.

A third large division that helps to characterize the various plot lines found in these novels distinguishes between those that motivate the seeking of a divorce by the desire for a second marriage and those that do not. If a second marriage is central to the motivation, the narrative will generally employ the two-suitor convention, with the unsatisfactory spouse figuring as one "suitor," the potential new mate as the alternative.[15] The bad spouse, it is important to emphasize, may be a thoroughly dangerous or abusive character—unfaithful, brutal, irresponsible, insane, or alcoholic. In Diehl's *The Confessions of Perpetua,* the bad spouse enters Perpetua's dreams in the form of raping giants and clawing demons: "I seem to have been dreaming—dreaming of pain unspeakable—of giants who fought me, then forcibly opened my mouth and poured fire down my throat —of little demons who sat upon me, grimacing, then tore my body with their hot steel claws" (276).[16] In *The Combined Maze,* Sinclair depicts the wrong mate as a manipulative wife, dishonest, irresponsible, and cruel to her children. In Cross's *The Life Sentence,* the wrong spouse is simply a December husband married to a May bride. As in the traditional two-suitor plot, the protagonist must go through a time of trial to sort out desires and duties. He or she must then negotiate his or her shift in loyalties with the community, here, very specifically, in the form of a confrontation with the law. In the euphoric version of the second-marriage plot, wedding bells are allowed to chime for the new and better marriage. In the dysphoric version, the second marriage is prevented and the novel's protest against current law is made.

In the conservative version of the second-marriage plot, the potential new mate may promise earthly bliss, but given the sinfulness of a second marriage while one's original spouse is still living, the new mate brings a poisoned pleasure. When the conservative novels do end happily, the suffering protagonist has resisted the lure of the better partner, stayed in the bad marriage, and seen the wrong spouse through to a natural death. Goodness is rewarded as duty *and* desire are fulfilled.

Many of the divorce novels do not motivate the plot with the desire for a second marriage, however. Instead, they set their characters off on the quest for a *decree nisi* with a range of motivations, from simple boredom to a growing recognition of their spouse's insanity or incurable alcoholism. Sexual betrayal is perhaps the most common motivation. One's mate has been unfaithful. The sense of insult is keen. How dare she? How dare he? Judgment upon the unfaithful partner, male or female, ranges from sympathy to condemnation. Several novels in this category carefully establish a background of mutual incompatibility. When wife or husband runs away with a lover, our sympathies can be divided between the spouse who escapes and the spouse who remains behind.

Beginning with a divorce or ending with one; arguing for or against liberalizing laws and procedures; focusing on wives, husbands, or couples; associating divorce with a second marriage or not: The Edwardian novel of divorce told its tale in many ways. The question before us now is how do the narratives that were spun by these novels relate to the narratives spun elsewhere? I have briefly indicated the way in which several of the novels explicitly dramatize issues being debated within the Royal Commission hearings, especially issues related to the adding of specific new grounds for a divorce. In what other ways do these novels reinforce, resist, or expand upon the conversation that surrounds them?

The divorce novel adds to the overall Edwardian debate in two significant ways. First, it provides insight into what Mary Ann Glendon sees as a central feature in most Westerners' attitude toward divorce, to wit, a feeling of complex ambivalence. To permit divorce seems at once threatening and essential to domestic order. To deregulate the process or to hedge it with a thicket of obstacles—the options seem both intelligent and ill-advised.[17] Second, the Edwardian divorce novel, in all of its variety, offers more, and more complex, plots, on three important issues: the proper role of communal surveillance with respect to marital failure; life after divorce; and the effect of divorce on children. I speak first to the novel's capacity to explore ambivalence.

In Chapter 1, I emphasized the way in which the tales told by the trial and the tabloids upheld the reigning narrative on divorce. Subsequently, in looking at the tales inspired by the hearings of the Royal Commission, I emphasized the opposite tendency, that is, the extent to which the hearings drew forth counterstories designed to undermine the reigning narrative. What is striking in the arena of the novel is the way in which stock stories challenge counterstories in a genuine debate. Whether conservative or reformist, all of these novels tend to be well crafted, with the density of detail that characterizes novels in general. For example, we do not find here the kind of skeletal sketch that a witness like Mrs. Steinthal brought to the Royal Commission hearings. Rather, we find balanced opposition as eloquent stock story speaks to eloquent counterstory.

Even more important, the quality of authentic debate exists not only among the novels but inside each novel as well, frequently revealing the ambivalence individual characters feel respecting divorce. As DuPlessis and others have argued, any lengthy novel maintains its drive "from the fundamental contradictions that animate the work" (3). Subtexts, conflicting stances, and repressed desires are the very stuff of "a linear form that must unroll in time" (3).[18] Recognizing this feature of fiction reminds us of the extent to which the speakers in a courtroom or at a hearing must address their audiences with at least the semblance of a coherent, consistent narrative. To get what they want, it is not in the interest of Clara Stirling, Cecil Chapman, or Lord Gorell, for example, to elaborate upon the many contradictions of motive, desire, or fact that crouch within the interstices of their stories. Such speakers must repress any ambivalence they may feel. By contrast, it is very much in the interest of the novelist to embroider the contradictions and ambiguities that keep readers reading, one page to the next. Because this tendency to explore contradiction and ambivalence is almost inherent in the novel as a genre, it shows up in the Edwardian divorce novel regardless of specific topic—though I see the tendency especially pronounced in the novels that deal with the effects of divorce on children. Let me turn now to the particular topics I have identified as new within the overall Edwardian conversation on divorce.

STOCK STORIES VERSUS COUNTERSTORIES

Communal Surveillance

In A. P. Herbert's influential novel of the 1930s, *Holy Deadlock,* the sorely besieged protagonists, Adam and Eve, lose their longed-for divorce after Eve's outburst in court. How can it be right for you—the law, press, and public—to pry into our affairs and judge us, she cries. You do not know us. You cannot know us. Up to that moment, the court seemed disposed to overlook the collusion it suspected and allow the divorce. But to question the propriety of its jurisdiction in deciding such matters at all—that was an inexcusable affront.

Each of the narrative arenas I have explored thus far has been highly public in its situation: a trial, a press story, a set of open hearings. Challenges were certainly mounted against the propriety of the press's involvement in divorce proceedings. But outrage against the involvement of the law itself—in the form of statutes, procedures, Lord Justices, barristers, solicitors, Royal Commissioners—this outrage is saved for the more private situation of the novel.

A novel of divorce, again by the definition I am using, moves its characters into the court system, consulting solicitors and barristers, hiring detectives, addressing judges, outfacing the public that is gathered in the courtroom and poring over the Sunday paper. In addition, it will often force its unhappy characters to go to spiritual or medical advisors, seek out parents, friends, siblings, colleagues. Explicitly or implicitly, conservative or reformist, the divorce novel in general undermines the assumption of marital privacy that has been a hallmark of traditional domestic fiction.[19] As indicated above, many of the most powerful of the divorce novels deplore the active role the community plays in marriage. But others celebrate the linkage, finding it natural, inevitable, and right. Much depends on how a particular novel defines "community."

Conservative divorce novels that see the communal gaze as inevitable or desirable often locate "community" less in the realm of secular law and more in the realm of divine and natural law. Moreover, the married couple is embedded in a society of concerned and watchful believers. Seen as a sacrament, marriage never was and never can be a private affair. One may appeal to secular laws in an effort to free oneself from the sacred bond and community, but such appeals are either futile or fatal.

For the lovely, long-suffering Flora and her potentially right mate in Cross's *The Life Sentence,* the futility is captured in the novel's title and closing lines: "It was all useless! We could not escape! It was the life sentence" (220). Addressing itself directly to the Church of England, Lucas Cleeves's *Woman and Moses* argues that neither death nor sin, including a wife's flagrant adultery, can break the bond that God has forged: "Even death," laments the divorced and guilt-ridden Arthur, "could not put asunder what God had joined" (299). To portray the breaking of the bond as fatal is often to call upon the forces of nature. In Mrs. Alexander's *The Crumpled Leaf: A Vatican Mystery,* the vast Catholic Church, including the pope himself, suggests the worldwide community that upholds the sacredness of every individual's marriage bond. When Lady Blanche Anson divorced her husband—however justifiably from a Protestant or secular perspective—she set herself against the community of the saved. Further, she cut herself off from nature itself. Till she repent, she is a withered, crumpled leaf, torn from the Tree of Life. Throughout *Daphne; or, Marriage a La Mode,* Mary Augustus Ward draws similar links between the marriage vow, divine sanction, the community of believers, and the awful powers of nature. Near the end of the novel, Ward calls on a force no less magnificent than the roaring Niagara Falls to represent all that stands behind the marriage contract.

Pro-reform novels can also valorize the presence of the community in marriage and divorce. Here, community is seen in the more down-to-earth shape of the intelligent solicitor or supportive family. The intent in these novels is often to demystify the practice of marriage. Often these texts will then proceed to claim nature and religion for the side of reform. As a petitioner, the rebellious spouse reads up on the statutes of the law, presents her or his case to a wise judge, and succeeds in the suit. *The Confessions of Perpetua* illustrates these dynamics well. Two months married to the possibly bigamous, certainly adulterous, Colonel Delincourt, the furious, terrified, and large-hearted Perpetua has two fathers to whom she can turn. On the one hand stands her dear but fanatically Catholic biological father; on the other, her calm and effective solicitor, Mr. Wittam. Perpetua's choice is not hard. Further supporting Perpetua as she extricates herself from the nightmarish Delincourt is a pair of aptly named women: her savvy sister, Florence, and the competent Nurse Magdalen. Helping Perpetua survive the months that precede her trial and then the months that must intervene between the *decree nisi* and *decree absolute,* this secular company, eventually joined by Flo's husband, is described as a cluster of nuns and monks in the best sense. With skill and competence, they devote themselves to helping another toward what the novel describes as a truly religious state of goodness, love, health, and happiness. Poised to be married in the end to Mr. Right, Perpetua closes her tale with a prayer: "Amen let it be! Thanks be to God—who loves us to be happy. Amen" (320). In *April Panhasard,* Muriel Hine similarly enlists community and religion in the fight for divorce. Awaiting her *decree absolute,* the stigmatized, shame-filled, and isolated April is finally tossed by the novel's plot at the foot of a cross in the flowery fields of Provence. There she gets her first clue that religion, properly understood, can release her from a paralyzing sense of loneliness and guilt. She moves forward and eventually remarries.

Putting a positive value on the communal gaze in a different way are the reformist novels concerned with the cost of divorce. Echoing the arguments heard throughout the hearings of the Royal Commission, *The Combined Maze, My Husband Still,* and *Mayfield* protest the financial obstacles that prevent the legal community from intervening in a scene of a marital disaster. In the first instance, Sinclair has John Ransome saving up for years to divorce the long since departed Violet, only to fail in the end. *My Husband Still* takes Minnie in and out of local magistrates' courts as she appeals for protection from her husband's violent returns and for maintenance money to support the children. Separation orders are within her reach; for financial reasons, divorce is not. *Mayfield* similarly focuses on the impossibility of divorce for the poverty-stricken wife of a criminal, adulterous, and abusive husband. In each case, the community, in the shape of the law, fails to come to the rescue. Communal surveillance is conspicuous in its absence.

However, many of the reform novels passionately resist the above invitation to greater surveillance. Seen mainly as secular law, the community is judged as utterly inadequate to the task of regulating something as complex and indecipherable as a marriage. As the shrewd and kindly lawyer in Galsworthy's *The Country House* advises old Horace Pendyce, "Don't let these matters come into court. If there is anything you can do to prevent it, do it. . . . Between personal delicacy and our law of divorce there is no relation; between absolute truth and our law of divorce there is no relation. I repeat, don't let these matters come into court. Innocent and guilty, you will all suffer; the innocent will suffer more than the guilty" (177). Indeed, "utterly inadequate" barely suggests the intensity of condemnation in, for example, Braby's *The Honey of Romance* or Bennett's *Whom God Hath Joined*.

In Braby's novel, the communal gaze is figured as a bunch of snooping detectives, querying the servants, crouching in the shrubbery, peering in the windows. Married nineteen years, thirty-nine-year-old Ernestine Trevor and her forty-three-year-old husband Robert mutually desire a divorce. For the most part, each is depicted as unhappy, hungry, and thoughtful.[20] And, as each realizes, they both have a good thirty years of life ahead of them. As Braby constructs their characters and the history of the marriage, she lays out the various ethical positions available to them as they plot out a collusive divorce within the context of each one's attraction to a younger mate.

Through the novel's long middle, the complicated legal maneuvering moves forward against Braby's persuasive depiction of all four adults, the Trevors and their lovers, approaching and avoiding each other. As the end of the novel draws near, the *decree nisi* is secured. A tense count-down follows as the foursome awaits the granting of the *decree absolute* that will allow all to remarry. But of course the *decree absolute* is denied. On a dark and stormy night, just before the promised release, Ernestine's lover takes refuge in her cottage. He conscientiously sleeps apart from her, but such niceties are lost on the spying detectives who have circled the house, acting in the service of the King's Proctor.[21] The novel closes on a cry of despair: "Oh! These English laws—the hideous cruelty and insanity of them! They drive us to sin—they force us" (248).

The Honey of Romance is sensational in its closing denunciation of the intrusiveness of the law. Bennett's *Whom God Hath Joined* denounces the legal gaze just as powerfully, but in a more thorough-going manner. He launches the novel with what he sees as the virtue of realistic fiction: its capacity to represent human affairs from a perspective sufficiently comprehensive to do them justice (1). His point: In the instance of divorce, the perspective of the law and press is insufficiently comprehensive and cannot possibly *do* justice. Beautifully designed, *Whom God Hath Joined* rehearses in detail the divorces of two couples in Five Towns, Lawrence and Phyllis Ridware and Charles and Alma Fearns. Lawrence seeks to divorce Phyllis for her adultery with Emery Greatbatch. Alma seeks to divorce Charlie for his adultery with their governess, Renee Souchon, and goodness knows how many other women over the years. "Cruelty" in the Fearn case will be legally provided by Charlie's adultery having occurred beneath the marital roof while Alma was away visiting her sister. In each case, the grounds for divorce are clear and indubitable, and in each case the law responds in the clumsiest of ways.

Chapter by chapter, Bennett's strategy is narrative replay. For example, in dramatizing Lawrence's discovery of Phyllis's affair, Bennett gives the reader a series of fully developed scenes conveying the complexities and sufferings within each character. He then has Lawrence, who is a solicitor, consult the office's dusty copy of Dixon's *Law and Practice in Divorce and Other Matrimonial Causes*. In listing what acts do and do not constitute grounds for a divorce, Dixon's language essentially rehearses what the scenes have depicted. However, moving "across the whole naked field of human suffering like a steam plough" (50), Dixon's legalistic approach is revealed as woefully inappropriate. Whether it be the paragraphs in Dixon; the "notes of evidence" provided by witnesses; the interviews between clients and solicitors; the lawyer to lawyer conversations; or the legal petitions submitted to the court: The language of the law is represented as "horrible" in its need to be curt, efficient, free of nuance, and unmarked by contradiction.

Horrible too is the language of the press. It deflates and inflates human suffering. Our first actual scene with Phyllis and Emery occurs after Lawrence has filed his petition. It is a highly emotional and effective moment in the text. We realize that Emery is now dying of diabetes, that they have indeed been lovers, and that this relationship has meant the world to them. Bennett then replays the fact of Emery's death as it is delivered by the press. The clerks in Lawrence's office read the brief death notice in the *Staffordshire Signal* and then hurry off to consult the indispensable Dixon. "It makes no difference to us," says clerk Pennington. The case will go on as planned. "Here it is on page 110. We've simply got to apply to have his name struck out; that's all" (162). In this instance, the press deflates. In the context of the trial scenes, it inflates.

Bennett's criticism of the communal gaze, as it operates within the court and press, culminates in the paired trial scenes. The Ridware trial is up first. Shifting his setting to dusky London and the ten thousand "lairs" that house the legal profession, Bennett reiterates his vision of the law as "destroying and never creating," as devoting itself to "the neat conclusion of disasters in proper form" (171). We walk with Lawrence along Chancery Lane, go over his case with the barrister in charge, and move on down the Strand to the Royal Courts of Justice. Dignified, ecclesiastical, and filled with a calm self-respect, these buildings are surely more representative of English justice. "Here," sighs the awed Lawrence, "is something pure; perhaps there is naught else so pure" (179). Lawrence has arrived early, so sits through the trials that precede his own. But as Carr *v.* Carr develops, Lawrence is shocked and disgusted. As he begins to perceive, "the secret imperious attraction of the Divorce Court" lies in its obligation and license to rehearse without reservation and in mixed company every lascivious detail of every act of fornication humans are capable of performing. "The animal in every individual could lick its chops and thrill with pleasure" (183). Once the descent and the wallowing have been sufficiently enjoyed, in steps the judge, saving the situation with his cool and penetrating judgment. Following the pattern, Lawrence's trial commences with titillating details of Phyllis's affair and then, surprisingly, introduces scandalous information on his own family history. This latter information, while highly entertaining to the audience and humiliating to Lawrence, turns out to be very significant to the judge. Owing to Lawrence's recent employ in Glasgow and to the circumstances of his birth (his parents were not yet married and his mother was Scottish), the petitions should have been filed in Scotland! Teasing this dazzling fact out of the evidence is a high point in the judge's day. Case dismissed.

The Fearn trial assumes the above critique and focuses on the Fearns' idealistic, intense, twenty-year-old daughter, Annunciata. It was she who discovered her father's adultery, she who must now testify as to what she saw. Throughout the months preceding the trial, Annunciata has maintained a proud composure. In anticipating the atmosphere of the court, she saw it as complementing her mein. It would be "arid, formal, awe-inspiring, almost supernatural" (227). When it is not—when the gossips from Five Towns become visible to her dazed eyes, when the judge and her father come into focus as ordinary humans—she is terror struck. She cannot speak. She flees the courtroom "like a wild deer" (227). Back in the corridor and in her mother's arms, she begs to go back in. No, says Mrs. Fearn. Requiring Annunciata to testify in public against her father was wrong. Alma drops the case, and they go home.

When the Fearn trial collapses, the press is at first dismayed. One of the assembled shorthand writers had been preparing himself to produce a report which we can only assume would have resembled the Stirling story. It "had been specially ordered by the *Staffordshire Signal* . . . [it] would appear piece by piece in successive editions of the daily organ of the Five Towns, under some such heading as 'Local Divorce Case: Astonishing Revelations'" (223). But the press recovers. With Annunciata's flight, the press has been given "that rare and thrilling phenomenon, beloved of all publics, a genuine 'scene in Court.' Within an hour or so, it was on the contents-bill of every evening paper in the three Kingdoms, including of course the *Staffordshire Signal*" (228).

Walking away from the adjourned trial, Lawrence's brother Mark Ridware and one of the solicitors from Five Towns argue about England's practice of divorce trials and unrestrained press coverage. Solicitor Cyples offers the stock story's standard defenses. Mark responds that the court cannot, by its very procedures, adequately deal with this kind of human suffering. As for the press, such coverage is far more likely to obstruct rather than facilitate justice. Witnesses back off, terrified by the publicity. Innocent and guilty alike become "marked" people. With respect to readers, the press coverage of divorce trials simply encourages their lascivious tastes.

Through this closing dialogue, Bennett is summing up his criticism of the entire trial and tabloid approach to divorce. How to deal with the failure of a marriage, be it the marriage of the Ridwares, Fearns, or indeed Stirlings? The courtroom and press adopt the conventions of the theater at its worst. Complex souls are positioned as actors and actresses in a script that must perforce center on sexual misdeeds. The long seasons and multiple sites of married life get reduced to a certain twenty-minute interval during which the defendant did or did not misconduct him- or herself with the corespondent. The trial must close with clear guilt and innocence. The tabloid report in turn must end on that stark note. Bennett's novel argues for a different approach to divorce, one that is, above all, better able to respect the nuances, ambiguities, and complexities of human relationships.

Bennett ends his own tale of divorce with a wrap-up. "The Solution" tells us that at much financial and psychic expense Lawrence succeeded in his suit in Scotland. Annunciata became a nurse. The enigmatic Phyllis went off to London to live her own life. The Fearn scandal died down, and Alma and Charlie's marriage gradually slipped back into its old shape. Element after element of the romance plot is refuted.[22] Phyllis, the adulteress, is neither punished, nor, owing to Bennett's manipulation of point of view, is she ever "exposed." She maintains her privacy.[23] The ascetic calm that Lawrence settles into is a good choice for him, and perhaps would have been all along. Most surprisingly, the beautiful Annunciata loves her work. Like many other young women, were they given the chance, Annunciata finds that her vocation taps into the seriousness, strictness, and inward fire that have always marked her character. Her celibacy is not presented as an unmixed blessing, as I discuss below, but it has its positive aspects. Free of sexual bonds, she has created a community for herself comprised of the people in her neighborhood and her extended family, excluding her father.

Life after Divorce

Bennett's post-divorce scenes are minimal; but many of the divorce novels take up life after divorce as a major concern of the plot. For Edwardians seeking to understand the nature of divorce, some vision of the months and years that follow upon the winning of a decree would appear useful. The stories told by trial and tabloid are no help. They end with the decree secured or denied. In the Royal Commission narratives, the focus is on issues that prevent people from ever getting to court in the first place.

By contrast, in the novels that grant their characters a divorce well before the end of the novel, a major interest is precisely the various challenges of the life ahead. For example, *The Soul of a Man* by Derek Vane and *The Cage Unbarred* by Gertie James open with restless wives. Each novel allows them to divorce early in the story and then sets the wives off on sexual adventures—in the former case, a second marriage. The plots develop so that each wife remarries her original partner, now happily. Set in South Africa, *A Mistaken Marriage* by F. E. Mills Young begins with Arthur Morrison marrying the good and sweet Sarah Lovall, recently arrived from England. After several years of degradation, Sarah is divorced by Arthur on trumped-up charges. Does she accept this decree? Indeed not. Living miserably as "neither maid, wife, nor widow" (349), Sarah basically denies the reality of the divorce. She remains true to her vows, refusing the love offered her by the worthy Michael Strange. H. G. Wells's *The New Machiavelli* opens with the narrator and his second wife in Italy, virtually exiled from their former, politically active life in England. It is the narrator's recent divorce that has sent them forth, seeking a new life and a clearer understanding of the old. Violet Hunt's *The Doll* and Bithia Mary Croker's *The Serpent's Tooth* trace the strained relations of divorced mothers and their daughters; in Philip Gibbs's *The Cus-*

tody of the Child, the focus is on a divorced father and his son. As noted above, in both *The Confessions of Perpetua* and *April Panhasard,* Diehl and Hine make much of the six-month probation that follows the heroine's *decree nisi.* Guy Thorne's *Divorce* features a former solicitor, the divorced woman he has wed, and the tragic consequences that follow upon their stigmatization. The censorious attitude of their neighbors is difficult but possible to withstand. But the Church of England's disinclination to allow them to receive communion is unbearable. Thorne's climax consists of the double suicide of this sensitive, passionately religious couple.

For all the variety and complexity of plot line, however, there is a tendency for most of the novels that explore the after effects of a divorce eventually to sound a note of either congratulation or condemnation and then elaborate on the gains or losses that divorce has brought. Ward's *Daphne; or, Marriage a La Mode* and Anthony Hope's *Mrs. Maxon Protests* are exemplary.

Opening *Daphne* in Washington, D.C., Ward distinguishes the respect for marriage one still finds in England from the lack of respect one finds in America— dear, dear America, so forward-looking and admirable in many ways, so deluded on this issue. But, Ward's novel predicts, the tide in America is turning. Her novel will do all it can to help.[24] Ward's message is clear. Through an American heroine and English hero, Ward denounces divorce on the grounds of religion, national interest, and humanitarian considerations. The bottom line is divorce goes against nature as those who practice it, individually or nationally, will find out.

But if the message is simple, the novel is not. Experienced writer that she is, Ward continually constructs sets of oppositions that she then problematizes in the woods of the narrative. The most obvious opposition pits bad Daphne Floyd against good Roger Barnes. A striking young woman, Daphne is Irish on her father's side, South American on her mother's. For all her cool sophistication, she has a Southern temperament, in particular, a streak of jealousy that is "volcanic and primitive" (83). Both parents being dead, she is on her own, an outspoken, ambitious heiress, used to getting her way with her very new money. Roger is from an old English family. He is Northern, fair, restrained, and tied to community values. Like other aristocratic families, the Barnes family has recently lost its old and venerable fortune. For Daphne to fall for Roger's particular blend of need and glamour; marry and move to England; be miserable there; flee back to America with their young daughter and buy a divorce in the infamous state of South Dakota: All of this is predictable. For the child to die; for Roger to be devastated; for Daphne gradually to lose her beauty as she is increasingly driven by egoistic ambition; and for her eventually to return to England in grief and remorse: This too is predictable. But there is more to the story.

Daphne is also a figure of twentieth-century youth, energy, and cosmopolitan views. As such, Ward sets her against Victorian age, complacency, bad taste, and provinciality. Settling into Roger's family home, Heston, Daphne continually fights with her mother-in-law in her desire to dismantle the ponderous and ornate redecoration scheme that has been imposed upon the home's original, clean, Adams designs. Daphne would restore Heston's eighteenth-century mantlepieces, clean the garishly retouched family portraits. And Daphne brings a degree of expertise, of real interest and education, to her task. For all her brashness and rudeness, she throws a spotlight on the Barneses' lack of education, smug assumptions, and tendency toward purposelessness. Ward makes clear that Daphne's jealousy of a former flame of Roger's, while extreme, reveals his inability to be perfectly honest, to confront unpleasantness. He temporizes. The more we know of him, the more we read in the Apollo-like beauty of his visage a vacuity, or, more accurately, the potential for vacuity. In these complexities and contradictions, Ward is making an obvious but important point, one that is again less easily made in a courtroom, press story, or parliamentary hearing: When a marriage falls apart, the causes are many, the parties complex. Is Ward also expressing a repressed argument here *for* divorce law reform, associating it with youth, energy, and a broad view of life? To some extent, yes. But as Ward shapes the densities that give substance to Roger and Daphne, her primary point is that Daphne—as woman, youth, and America—must pour her energies into the betterment of Roger—as needful male and representative of the struggling but precious Old World. As she has tackled Heston, with the desire to restore it to its former beauty, so Daphne should tackle Roger, drawing forth the true, firm, active squire that resides within his bones and breeding.

The subplot Ward develops around the tale of Daphne's good friend, Madeleine Verrier, also complicates the novel's primary dualisms. Exposition on Madeleine Verrier tells us that she is from a well-connected New York family and fell in love three years ago with Leopold Verrier, a Jew. She married him. Her community turned against her, and her family set about breaking up the marriage. Madeleine tried to keep up her old friendships, often going alone to affairs to which Verrier had not been invited. Isolated and unhappy, she began thinking about divorce. After one of many interviews with Madeleine's mother, however, Verrier went up to Niagara Falls and committed suicide. Moving through most of the novel as Daphne's advocate, Madeleine gradually stops denying her part in Verrier's death and eventually withdraws her support of Daphne's divorce. By the end, Madeleine is fixated on the site of Leopold's suicide, wasting away within the sound of Niagara's judgmental voice. While this subplot reinforces the message that divorce, in contemplation or actuality, wrecks havoc on everyone it touches, Madeleine's tale also undermines a too easy identification of marriage with family, of divorce with the desire to strike out on one's egoistic own. Madeleine's marriage took her away from her family. Her contemplated divorce was designed to return her to her people and her community.[25]

The complex characterization of Roger and Daphne and the Verrier subplot are two of many ways Ward enriches the ultimately conventional stock story she delivers on divorce. On one issue, however, she gives the reader a consistent line of conservative argument throughout. Daphne is a feminist. In this, she is wrong, wrong, wrong. She may believe herself to be engaged in the fight for justice, but committing herself to feminist causes is an unnatural activity that will yield no satisfactory results. Further, feminism is positively harmful in leading to the skyrocketing divorce rates in America. What is so hard for the right-thinking, anti-divorce characters in the novel to understand is why so many American women, Daphne among them, walk away from marriage without a second marriage in mind. If it is not for another over-mastering love, then such a desertion must be "in the interests . . . of what women call 'their individuality.'" And what is that? "A whim, a nothing" (258).

Rubbish, says Anthony Hope. To turn from *Daphne* to the aptly named *Mrs. Maxon Protests* is to be struck again by the courageous way many of these novels address the surrounding debate but also by the extent to which the divorce novels talk to each other. Published two years after *Daphne, Mrs. Maxon Protests* takes on a key issue being debated within the ongoing hearings of the Royal Commission—wifely adultery—while it explicitly addresses Ward's well-known stance on feminism.[26] As does Ward, Hope builds his plot around the divorce and subsequent experiences of a restless young wife. Echoing Ward, Hope sets up an opposition between the claims of community and self, and then complicates that opposition. But for him, Winnie Maxon's decision to divorce Cyril Maxon is admirable. Her feminism is a gradually developing philosophy, powerfully linked to personal experience as well as to a range of opposing philosophies. As Hope traces out the years that follow Winnie's divorce, he explicitly plays off Ward's opening allusion to Odysseus and Penelope, identifying Winnie as Odysseus and her old friend, Dick Dennehy, as Penelope. Hope does this partly by refiguring the image of the house that plays through so much of the Edwardian rhetoric on divorce, including the rhetoric in *Daphne*.[27]

In *Daphne,* the first house we encounter is Mount Vernon, the second is the White House. Each represents a perfect domicile, youthful in its American energy yet dignified in its Old World values, particularly as those values relate to wifely loyalty. At Mount Vernon, that loyalty is conveyed through the tale of Martha Washington's decision to withdraw to one of the backrooms after George Washington's death, there to mourn him by gazing out at his tomb. Replicating this act at Niagara becomes the project of the grieving Madeleine. At the White House, vibrant and bustling with democratic ideals, the Old World values are captured in Ward's description of President and Mrs. Theodore Roosevelt as the brave Odysseus and loyal Penelope. Had Daphne committed herself to Roger and Heston, she could have recreated there a site as lovely as Mount Vernon, the White House, or the palace at Ithaca. Choosing not to, Daphne is set adrift, alone, living out of suitcases, empty of true purpose.

With the odd word "inkpat," Hope opens his novel not in a home but a lawyer's office. Winnie Maxon has come to ask Hobart Gaynor if she may, under the law, leave her respectable home and her domineering barrister husband for nothing more nor less than incompatibility. The word itself she has shortened, feeling that it is both too long to call up as often as she requires and too "impartial." Creating her own word is a first step toward asserting her own understanding of who she is and what has gone wrong. "Broadly speaking," she says, "inkpat's a demand that a woman should be not what she is, but a sort of stunted and inferior reproduction of the man. . . . Anything that's not like that gets inkpatted" (3). Gaynor tells her that she may legally leave her home and marriage. Maxon may sue her for restitution of conjugal rights but she may then refuse to return. He can choose to give her no money, but with her small independent income, she can just manage. Given that no adultery has occurred, Winnie's desertion will give Cyril grounds for a formal separation, although not a divorce. Winnie is pleased. She packs up, asserting the claims of the eager, hungry self: "She had only one life—that was the unspoken plea of her youth, her beauty, and her new born zest in living" (66).

Immediately, Hope counters Winnie's claims with those of Cyril and his spiritual advisor, Reverend Francis Attlebury. Holding to the high doctrine of duty to others, they agree that Cyril himself must stay true to the ideals of church and state. Although Winnie may leave him, he will not leave her. The marriage will not be broken. The door of their house will stay open to her. When she finally comes back home, ashamed and asking for forgiveness, it will be a refuge.

So where does egoistic Winnie go? Not on a journey out of the marital home and on to the open road, but on a journey that follows a rhythm of exits and entrances, of going in and out of houses, of being with friends, communities, a new mate, and alone. Her first destination is Shaylor's Patch, home of her skeptical cousin Stephen Aikenhead and his wife, Tora. The Aikenhead community takes her in and nurtures her, mentally and materially. From there she links up with Godfrey Ledstone, soon moving with him into a flat in Kensington. But Godfrey's shocked family draws him back to their respectable home in Wobern Square. Winnie is now alone in the Kensington flat, hating it for its painful memories and unable, in any case, to manage the rent on her own. Cyril, in the meantime, has initiated divorce proceedings, based on Winnie's adultery with Ledstone and his own interest in marrying again.

Enter old, courageous, and scandalous Mrs. Lenoir. Won't Winnie come and keep her company in her house in Knightsbridge and then join her for a sojourn in Madeira and Italy? Winnie will. Months later, back in Knightsbridge, Winnie is again alone and without a house. She has neither inherited the now-deceased Mrs. Lenoir's residence nor secured a marriage with conventional Bertie Merriam. As she is beginning to see things, she is indeed free—the divorce with Cyril is a fait accompli—but over the months and years, her life has become a repetitious pattern of entering and exiting relationships and houses. She wants to settle down.

It never occurs to her that she should return to Cyril. Should she return to Shaylor's Patch? The Aikenheads say come. Stephen is about to launch a large research project. He wants to write *The Synopsis of Social Philosophy*. Drawing on every kind of past thinker— from philosophers to poets to playwrights—the synopsis will include ideas on education, private property, marriage, divorce, women, and labor. It will be shaped by a belief that all sides to any real issue have a lot to say for themselves (318). Becoming ever more "a student of human nature" (211), Winnie would be the perfect colleague. The Aikenheads will get her cottage cleaned and whitewashed. The rent is affordable. Winnie assents. In choosing to settle among the jolly, argumentative community at Shaylor's Patch, Winnie selects one of those alternative human bonds that DuPlessis sees as so crucial in undermining the constricting conventions of the romance plot.

But as indicated above, the novel does not end here. In the very last chapter, Hope gives his Odysseus her Penelope. This ending can be read as either a last-minute capitulation to the romance plot or an unstable closure to a courageous counterstory on divorce and female independence. For me, it reads as the latter. Having established herself as brave, thoughtful, experienced, and inquiring, Winnie seems to get it all, a community of intellectually challenging friends and a loving mate. At the same time, by titling the last chapter "Is This the Result?" Hope continues to question the conventional. Hope's last words on Winnie emphasize an open future. Winnie remains one who "raise[s] questions in unquestioning people," whose "management of her life put them on inquiry as to the familiar" (361). Significant also is Hope's repeated description of the house that Winnie and Dick will live in. It was designed and built by the Aikenheads. It is a stone's throw from their place. To marry is not to withdraw into some private realm. Marriages are lived out in proximity to others and in the spaces they have designed for us.

In *Mrs. Maxon Protests,* Hope sets against each other the incompatible theories of the novel's large cast of characters. He then sets all of those theories against the detailed, changing experiences of his protagonist. In the end, the only philosophy that holds up is the one captured by Stephen's projected book: The truth is "in solution." In her journey as a divorced woman, Winnie has demonstrated that the presumed dichotomies of yearning self and censorious community, of one home and no home, of respectable behavior and scandalous rebellions are too simple.

The Haunting Child

In *Regulating Divorce,* Eekelaar looks back at the Edwardian debate and analyzes the way the problem of divorce was "officially conceived" (23). In his view, the official conception focused on permanently separated adults who were unable to remarry. While I see a greater range of problems being formulated—from female poverty, to freedom of the press, to women's participation in the judicial process—Eekelaar is right in pointing out the relative invisibility of children. Some commissioners and witnesses spoke to the effect of divorce on the child, but the official conception of the problem had its sight set on adults. As for the visibility of children within the negotiations of the divorce trial and resulting press stories, children were seen as ancillary.

At first, the same relative invisibility seems to characterize the novels. Of the thirty-six novels considered here, only six develop what would seem a predictable plot under any circumstance but especially given the model provided in 1897 by James's *What Maisie Knew*. Husband and wife split; children are then divided between parents or are reared by a single parent; argument is made for or against this reconfiguration of the family. Croker's *The Serpent's Tooth* works with this material, as do *My Husband Still,* Scott's *The Caddis Worm,* Sinclair's *The Combined Maze,* Gibbs's *The Custody of the Child,* and Hunt's *The Doll.* In *The Serpent's Tooth,* the heroine divorces her brutal husband and devotes years of her life to maintaining her young daughter. The daughter is cold and ungrateful; the mother eventually breaks free and remarries. In *The Caddis Worm,* compliant Catharine, mother of six, leaves her dictatorial husband, fights for her right to have a say in the children's futures, and dismally contemplates what the children's modest life with her would be in contrast to a more sumptuous life with their father. Betrayed and deserted John Ransom in *The Combined Maze* moves in with his struggling parents as he tries to manage child care for his two young children and save for a divorce. Minnie, in *My Husband Still,* cannot even imagine saving enough, as she too struggles to rear her two children after her husband decamps. *The Doll* is discussed below.

In one of the most poignant of the six novels mentioned above, *The Custody of the Child,* young Nicholas Barton watches his writer father "Bristles" divorce his actress mother "Beauty" over his mother's lover, "The Beast." Through much of the novel, Gibbs does a beautiful job creating the perspective of Nicholas. As a youngster, he is confused: Bristles got a "decree nicely"? What does that mean? Growing up, Nicholas is angry, guilt-ridden, and above all torn. Loving his loyal, struggling father, he nevertheless longs for his glamorous, absent mother. In its concluding scenes—those moments in the narrative when a simplistic ideological solution can be imposed on the fundamental contradictions that have carried the tale thus far—*The Custody of the Child* inveighs mightily against all divorce and the pain that wicked women bring to long-suffering men. Up until that bitter turn, however, we have a novel explicitly pledged to search for "the truth." It is the task that Gibbs gave to Nicholas at the novel's outset, and it "kept him busy . . . truth was always playing hide and seek" (10).

These novels aside, however, the remainder seem again to focus solely on adults and their quarrels with themselves, others, the law, and the press. Then variations on a line tug at the memory. This happened before, or after, the baby died. Of course it would have been different if the baby had lived. Oh dearest, remember how we cried when the baby died. Surely things would have gone better if we had been able to have children. In fact, once we begin looking for them, children are everywhere in the Edwardian novels of divorce, haunting the woods of the narrative, complicating the plots. They float through the texts as the dead or never born. Equally fascinating, they are there as the grown and troubled.[28]

That a chorus of dead or never-conceived children should figure somewhere in the conservative novels is hardly surprising. Whether it is the briefly mentioned dead baby in Alexander's *The Crumpled Leaf* or the long-suffering, dying child in *Daphne,* the linkage between divorce and the blasting of the next generation is predictably made. Any nation that is wrongheaded enough to open the doors to divorce invites precisely this blight. Any individual who opens that door will bear upon his or her conscience the crime of child murder. The closing image of Ward's bereft and sobbing Daphne says it all.

However, dead children also haunt the novels that campaign for *liberalizing* divorce. Out of nowhere comes the image: the baby that Winnie Maxon lost; the beautiful and lively young boy killed in a hunting accident in *April Panhasard;* sweet baby Yvonne, still mourned by estranged Robert and Ernestine in *The Honey of Romance.* In *The Confessions of Perpetua,* we look into the coffin of the illegitimate daughter of Colonel Delincourt and we hear of Perpetua's aborted child, lost during her bout with diphtheria. Into these often high-spirited, pro-reform novels, the dead children slip in and out, attached to the plot in what seem the most tenuous of ways.

But of course they are deeply attached to the plot, as are the grown children analyzed below. When Robert

Scholes writes of the ways a novel interrogates its own dualisms, he emphasizes in particular the tracing of "the ever restless voice within," of the activity of consciousness as conscience.[29] If novels may be said to bear within their very bones an ethical paradigm, it is, Scholes argues, the paradigm of inner questioning. As I read these references to dead babies and children, again especially in the novels that argue *for* divorce, I see them signaling a wide spectrum of tensions and ambivalences. At one and the same time, the dead babies and children express the restless adult's fears and guilts respecting the damage he or she is doing to innocent others. They convey a concern that divorce may actually do harm to the nation's future population. They serve as a subtle reminder of the marriage's initial intimacy. And they figure the wish to be free of domestic responsibilities and ties. The dead and the never-conceived are, in brief, emblems of past pleasure, current desire, guilt, and fear. And what of the grown children?

Entering these novels like adult versions of James's little Maisie, the older children bring years of pent-up questioning, yearning, resentment. They too figure guilts, fears, wishes—their own and those of their parents—but also sexual confusions and complexities.

In Mrs. Dudeney's *The Third Floor,* the heroine's birth occurred simultaneous with her parents' divorce. Valencia Dorrell's mother was given custody, but for a variety of selfish and well-meant reasons, she had Valencia brought up in foster homes and boarding schools and gave her a pseudonym—taken significantly from a newspaper account of a woman who committed suicide because she had too many children. As the novel opens, Valencia is a questing young adult who has begun to suspect that she is not in fact an orphan; she asks over and over, "Who am I?" "Where do I belong?" She feels like a stray cat. The idiot-savant Paul Stilling, in Harraden's *Interplay*, is equally confused about where he belongs. He lives with his stepmother, who loves him very much in spite of her divorce from his father. Perceiving that she has a chance to remarry, the gentle Paul agonizes that he is in the way, that by his very existence he is a reminder of her past and an obstacle to her life's moving forward. Other grown children find themselves playing and replaying the moment of the family breakup. Often they see themselves as having caused the rupture and then as having been torn from one parent and forced to live with the other. The parent who disappeared is idealized and imagined to be endlessly hungering for the child who was snatched away. The parent who remains is the imperfect quotidian. The child is grateful to the caregiver, but keeps longing for the breach to disappear, for all to be made whole again. Hunt's *The Doll* explores these issues with unusual optimism.

On the morning of her twenty-first birthday, bright, hard, and shiny Miss Isabel Agate marches out into the streets of London to track down her mother. Isabel is portrayed as a huntress; notably erect, she stands five feet nine in her hunting boots (19). Finding her mother is not, however, all that difficult as Minnie Hawtayne is a well-known novelist and suffragette. Isabel has been keeping tabs on her through the newspapers ever since the Agates' divorce fourteen years earlier. Isabel sees herself leaving behind all of the unhappiness of her childhood, with its memories of being torn from her mother, watching her uncommunicative father die, and living with an unsympathetic stepmother. She is about to return to where she should have been all along. Her brave, strong mother will be good. Her new father will be kind. They will be Darby and Joan, but with a sophisticated glow about them. Their house, as she knows from the society pages of the papers, is a brilliant center of lively conversation. Diplomats and politicians, lords and ladies gather there. From out of its portals, Isabel intends to launch herself into society and her own brilliant marriage. In the end, Isabel is launched from her mother's house, but it takes the entire length of the novel to get her ready.

Isabel reaches Cortachy Gardens, knocks, is shown in, and then waits. And waits. An unconscionable amount of time passes as she nervously attempts to find out something about her mother through contemplation of her mother's study. The place is a shambles. All kinds of people lounge about. There are photographs of men everywhere. Who are they? Which is her stepfather? Who is the little boy? There is whispering in the corridor that Minnie Hawtayne is still not up. Minnie's personal secretary eventually comes in and, not knowing who Isabel is, begins to gossip. The goings-on in this house! Miss Clutton tells of Mrs. Hawtayne's having an affair, of Ralph Hawtayne's jealousy and anger, of the entire house being ruined by promiscuity, alcohol, and drugs. When Minnie eventually comes in, she tells Isabel to leave. Cortachy Gardens is not the right home for her; she, Minnie, is not the right mother. Indeed, she is "a black bat that is used to dark corners" (97).

Isabel leaves but keeps coming back. As Isabel meets the other inhabitants of this unhappy house, Miss Clutton's gossip takes on credibility. Pervading the house is an atmosphere of anger. Young Lord Precelly certainly

acts the part of her mother's lover. Her stepfather is undeniably miserable. His and Minnie's child, Timothy, is
a forlorn figure, clinging tightly to a torn and filthy as-
semblage of rags wrapped around a stick. This is his
doll, full of disease and dirt, explicitly used as an em-
blem of human error and misrule. A second divorce
seems in the offing.

The misunderstandings that already abound in this
house flourish with the arrival of Isabel. In one of his
darkest moments, Ralph has a horrifying vision of Isabel, Minnie, and Lord Precelly all living and sleeping
together in an incestuous triangle. His dear little Timothy will wander through the place dragging after him
his fetish to filth.

Sorting out the confusions and discovering the complicated but largely decent truths becomes the task of
the family friend, Taplin. Through Taplin, Hunt ex-
poses the extremity of Minnie's feminist stance against
marriage and against a father's legitimate interest in his
children. At the same time, Taplin argues Ralph out of
his assumption that a respectable house must be a closed
house. Minnie's delight in an open house is seen as
good. Most important, Hunt expands the reader's sense
of what divorce can mean to a child. For Isabel, it is an
education. When she began her journey, Isabel was na-
ive and opinionated, in no way ready to come out and
contract her own marriage. Studying her mother's divorce and difficult remarriage has transformed her.
Hunt captures what Isabel has learned in the new doll
Taplin gives to Timothy. It is not the kind of idealized
prince or silly sailor Timothy has rejected in the past.
But neither is it a tangle of disease-ridden rags. Rather,
it is a great grand "golliwog," black, comely, gro-

tesque, and clean.[30] As Timothy's rags are tossed in the fire, the novel urges the reader to forget past representations of marriage and divorce, ones that force a choice between the demonic and the ideal.

Among the things Isabel learns about the glamourous Minnie is that she has never, in fact, been especially interested in sexual relations. She is passionate about friends, ideas, and young children. Many of the grown children, struggling with their parents' divorce, fare less well than Isabel, partly because their parents' sexuality is played up rather than down. In these novels, the frightening image Ralph Hawtayne has of daughter, mother, and lover all sleeping together comes to the fore. Because novels of divorce open the sexual life of the couple to the gaze of a community that includes the couple's children, and because the sexual activity associated with divorce is illicit, divorce novels often force children to confront their parents' illicit sexual desires—and parents to confront the same in their children. In these novels, there is a remarkable lifting of the curtain respecting the confusing and illicit sexual desires of parents and children.

The most moving sequence in Galsworthy's *The Country House* is the journey that the dignified Marjorie Pendyce makes into London to promote the love affair of her smitten son George and Mrs. Helen Bellew. Knowing full well that a divorce between the Bellews, with George named as corespondent, will break up the Pendyce family, she works nevertheless for that divorce out of her love for George. Walking out on her husband, who has threatened to disown George, Mrs. Pendyce tracks George down like a lover. She leaves notes at his club, begs him to come to her hotel. Identifying with his desires, she has slipped out of her role as respectable wife and longs to insinuate herself into George's affair. When Marjorie discovers that Helen Bellew has lost all interest in George, she takes over Helen's role. She goes to George's flat, makes him let her in, forces him to cling to her, to cry. Marjorie combats George's suicidal despair by making him respond to her love. When she leaves, George gives her the jewels that Helen had just returned.

In Galsworthy's novel, the focus is on a parent forced into an acute awareness of her bluff and distant son's sexual vulnerability and desires. In more of the novels, the focus is reversed. Time and again, the grown child is forced to recognize the ungovernable sexual appetites of his or her mother or father. In Bennett's *Whom God Hath Joined,* the idealistic Annunciata must confront her father's adultery. Doing so precipitates a premature identification with betrayed women, her mother in particular. With no life experience to help her understand her father, she is far more horrified than is Mrs. Fearns. As indicated above, Bennett's closing scene does help expand the future options available to intense, ascetic young women, but in Annunciata's case, the devotion to service is undeniably linked to arrested sexual development. Nicholas Barton, in *The Custody of the Child,* is far younger than Annunciata when his mother begins her affair with "The Beast," but in his late adolescence, when he finally succeeds in locating her, her promiscuities similarly check his own developing sexuality.

The Caddis Worm dramatizes this exposure of parental sexuality differently. Eminent and middle-aged, Dr. Robert Blake discovers his idolized mother's passionate past and his own illegitimacy. He is furious. But she fights back. "Mothers aren't human, are they? We aren't to live our lives, we are to remember we may have children and that they will expect us to have no histories" (278). She charges him with his own past, saying, "Believe me, one generation is as like the last as peas in a pod, and what I did yesterday, you do today, and your children will do tomorrow" (278). The scene ends with them holding hands and talking of people who live in glass houses.

For other grown children, the parents' sexuality enters the tale in the form of an intergenerational competition. Yearning for renewed youth, the mother or father woos the child's peers. In *The Honey of Romance,* Robert Trevor wants luscious young Anita Mountjoye; Ernestine Trevor wants beautiful young Dorian de la Pasque. The Trevors' grown son Bobby is away on assignment with the navy, but he haunts his parents' affairs. Why, thinks Ernestine, Dorian is practically the age of Bobby. Why, thinks Robert, it is Bobby who should be marrying Anita. In Howell's *Mrs. Charteris,* young doctor Paul Charteris watches in dismay as his mother woos his sister Gertrude's potential suitor, who is also Paul's own good friend. Julia Charteris is ruthless. Turning her back on the dying Paul, maneuvering her daughter out of the way, she *will* have her second chance at life, love, youth.

The Edwardian divorce novel emerges alongside other problem novels of the decade as a lively, thoughtful, and well-crafted text, committed to ventilating taboo topics and resisting the immediately preceding tendency in popular fiction toward escapism. The divorce novel also converses with the surrounding narratives on divorce in complex ways. One can imagine the amused reader of the Divorce Court page in the penny tabloid deeming the divorce novels tiresome in their sheer length and overly subtle in their complex plots. To witnesses who came before the Royal Commission with a strong interest in divorce and the working class, the divorce novels must have appeared narrowly middle class in orientation. And yet I would say these novels, by virtue of their very length, complexity, and even middle-class focus, extended the Edwardian conversation on divorce in important ways. I have spoken of the novel's capacity to reveal over time the ambiguities inherent in most failing marriages, the ambivalence felt as to the potential gains and losses of divorce. I have spoken too of the fresh territory explored in the novels, from the fundamental propriety of the community's interest in marriage and divorce, to life after divorce, and the effect of divorce on children. In addition, one notes that these novels reached out to a readership that was admittedly smaller than the tabloids' vast audience but still significant in size and bound to be influential in creating the reforms that eventually would occur over the next decades.

Here let me summarize specific insights about wives, husbands, and marriage found in these novels, insights that further added to the conversation on divorce and emerged as the novels explored the fresh territory named above. To a surprising extent, the pro-reform novels offer a cast of wives who go to law without unsexing themselves, refuse to be identified in any simple way with an exclusive or impermeable marital home, and commit adultery without punishment. Conversely— and here the conservative novels join in—these narratives deliver a cast of husbands whose identities are strongly linked to domesticity. Husbands like Lawrence Ridware, Roger Barnes, and John Ransome continually take the pulse of their marriage, now hopeful, now brooding. They replay old quarrels, invest mightily in possible rapprochements, and think longingly of the past.

If, more than in the courtroom, press, or even Royal Commission hearings, wives and husbands in the novels can appear in roles that challenge the assumption of separate spheres found in most of the stock stories, it is also true that in the novels the ending of a marriage appears in a different light than elsewhere. More than in the other arenas, the novels offer the insight that a divorce may mark no simple ending, perhaps no ending at all. Often the bonds continue to haunt, linger, press, sometimes like a life sentence.

In *Edwardian Stories of Divorce,* I have explored a range of narratives inspired by an historical debate over an issue that continues to trouble England and its neighbors. At the very least, I hope I have suggested the richness of the Edwardians' conversation. On this issue, they were not innocents. The reigning tale was produced by the highly publicized divorce trial. Its message was clear: Marriage should be forever. Only upon proof of a grave offense and at high psychological and financial cost could it be dissolved. The clouds of narrative, of *petits recits* in Jean-François Leotard's words, that rose up to challenge that narrative did what resisting narratives generally do: spun out a wide array of alternative plots and images.[31] As Raymond Carver might ask, what did Edwardians talk about when they talked about divorce?[32] In their trials they talked about adultery, but also about justice, discipline, and responsibility. They talked about how one gets at the truth of a marriage. In their tabloids, they talked about glamour and squalor. Using a style that alternately inflated and deflated, the tabloid tales highlighted the glitter of aristocratic adultery—where it occurred and how it was costumed—while they simultaneously represented scenes of quotidian adultery as squalid and ridiculous: a horse-trading husband who acts as pimp; a mistress by the name of Spittle. Writ large or small, in the tabloids divorce was represented as frequent, worthy of publicity, and linked to crime and theater.

When witnesses to the Royal Commission talked about divorce, they talked about offenses that went beyond adultery and sufferings that were associated partly with the very rules that governed storytelling in the courtroom and press. In constructing counterstories about the dissolving of marriage, they talked about violence, desertion, venereal disease, alcoholism, and insanity; about eugenics; about the working class and the position of women; about England's masculine approach to justice.

Novel writers, reformist or conservative, responded to all of the above with tales that reinforced both stock story and counterstory. Set within the middle-class and designed to appeal to middle-class buyers, these tales talked less about domestic violence and/or economic bars to divorce and more about female self-determination and male domesticity; the community's intimate involvement in marriage; an individual's internal struggles, longings, doubts, and disquiets; the confusions that divorce visits on parents and children; and the naiveté of anyone thinking that marital ties, even after a divorce, will necessarily cease to bind.

If in the end we cannot find one or two all-encompassing, capital-letter words to sum up what Edwardians talked about when they talked about divorce,[33] we can recognize that they set the terms for the twentieth-century conversation and did so with a good deal of prescience.

Many of these Edwardian storytellers were able to imagine a practice of divorce that would move beyond the concept of marital offense—with one person guilty, one innocent—and uphold the more ambiguous concept of marital breakdown. Some foresaw the church and state withdrawing from the field, ceasing to declare any special interest in keeping a dying marriage alive. Neither Braby nor Bennett predicted the current practice of allowing divorcing parties to fill out a form and mail it in through the post office, but one suspects they might have approved. A few Edwardians saw women actively participating in the creation of new procedures. Many predicted the steep rise in the rates of divorce that has in fact characterized the century, and some foresaw the feminization of poverty that has accompanied this rise, especially in England and the United States. Some foresaw simultaneously that in the eyes of many women, forbidding divorce was no way to address the economic inequities that exist between men and women. And finally, some foresaw the extent to which an issue defined as "ancillary" at the beginning of the century would become central at century's end: the need to think in more complex ways about divorce and children. Taken as a group, Edwardians saw that on divorce there would be no easy story.

Recommendations
of the Royal Commission

Your Lordship,
    I am taking the liberty of writing you to ask you if you could let me know if I am a free woman, as I am leaving for South Africa next Saturday. . . .

Yours obediently,

—*Report of the Royal Commission* 4, appendix 26: 186

Edwardians expressed feelings of urgency not only about the actual legal changes they desired but about when those changes would occur. Taking the short view, one can say that many of the reforms recommended by the commission were agonizingly slow in coming. An Edwardian wife or husband deserted in 1912, for example, would languish another twenty-five years before she or he could apply for a decree. Justice for all, rich and poor alike, came haltingly, with the barriers related to cost addressed through a series of gradual changes in legal aid regulations. Not until 1949 could a woman like the one whose letter introduces Chapter 2 claim genuine access to the divorce court. But there is also a long view. Within two generations, England officially redefined its fundamental position on the breakdown of a marriage and transformed itself from a nation that was anomalous for its low rates of divorce to one that is anomalous for its high rates.

The following offers an overview of the recommendations for change made by the Royal Commission in its report of 1912 and subsequent responses. As indicated above, the focus here is more on changes in the divorce law, less on changes in the Separation Acts or declaration of a null marriage.

Questions
I. Should any, and, if any, what courts have jurisdiction to hear and determine divorce and other matrimonial causes, at any, and, if any, at what places, in addition to the High Court sitting in London?
II. What should be the extent of such jurisdiction, and what procedure should be adopted?
III. Should any, and, if any, what alterations be made with regard to the exercise of the jurisdiction conferred by the Summary Jurisdiction (Married Women) Act, 1895, and the provisions of the Licensing Act, 1902, relating to separations in cases of habitual drunkenness?
IV. Are any, and, if any, what amendments of the said Acts of 1895 and 1902, and of the procedure and practice thereunder desirable?
V. Should the law be amended so as to place the two sexes on an equal footing, as regards the grounds upon which divorce may be obtained?
VI. Should the law be amended so as to permit of divorce being obtained on any, and, if any, what grounds, other than those at present allowed?
VII. Are any other, and if any other, what amendments needed in the law, procedure and practice relating to divorce, nullity of marriage, and other matrimonial questions?
VIII. Should any, and, if any, what provisions be made for preventing or limiting the publication of reports of divorce and other matrimonial cases? (*Report of the Royal Commission* 4, pt. 7:29)

The majority—Gorell, Balfour, Burt, Guthrie, Treves, Tindal-Atkinson, Tennant, Brierley, and Spender—express their views on these questions.

RECOMMENDATIONS OF THE ROYAL COMMISSION

It will be observed that the first four questions are concerned with the administration of the law, though they may in some respects involve amendments of the existing law, while the next three deal mainly with alterations in the existing law, and only incidentally with improvements in the present procedure and practice. The last question may be regarded separately.

We have considered the questions with the anxious desire that any recommendations we might make should be of a nature to strengthen, and not to weaken, the national character, to promote the highest possible standard of morality for both sexes and of regard for marriage and family life, and the best interests of society and the State; and that they should provide for the administration of justice in matters with which the inquiry is concerned, in such a way that adequate means should be available for all classes of the community to bring their cases before the courts of justice. (*Report of the Royal Commission* 4, pt. 7: 29)

Here the majority proceeds to define the principles upon which their recommendations were made, to review the testimony of witnesses, and then to take each question, break it down into a series of subquestions, and construct detailed recommendations. They conclude with the following "Conspectus."

The recommendations, made in this Report and summarised above, may be conveniently grouped under the following heads, which show in general terms what is proposed:—
1. The decentralization of sittings for the hearing of divorce and matrimonial cases to an extent sufficient to enable persons of limited means to have their cases heard by the High Court locally.

2. The abolition of the powers of Courts of Summary Jurisdiction to make orders for the permanent separation of married persons and the introduction of amendments with regard to their powers, procedure, and practice.

3. The placing of men and women on an equal footing with regard to grounds for divorce.

4. The addition of five grounds for divorce which are generally recognized as in fact putting an end to married life. [In addition to the existing ground of adultery, the added grounds were specified as desertion for three years and upwards; cruelty; incurable insanity after five years' confinement; habitual drunkenness found incurable after three years from first order of separation; imprisonment under commuted death sentence. See vol. 4, "Summary," 163.]

5. The addition of grounds for obtaining decrees of nullity of marriage in certain cases of unfitness for marriage.

6. The introduction of other amendments of the present law, procedure, and practice in a number of details. [Among the recommendations here is the abolishing of juries in divorce trials.]

7. The making of certain provisions with regard to the publication of reports of divorce and matrimonial cases. [Here the majority specified that a judge be able to close the court for the whole or part of a case "if the interests of decency, morality, humanity, or justice so require"; that the judge be able to prohibit publication of portions of a case deemed "unsuitable" "in the interests of decency or morality"; that no reporting occur until after a case has been concluded; that all pictorial representations be prohibited; that any person infringing upon the above suggestions be liable for contempt of court. See vol. 4, "Summary," 165.]

8. The extension of the protecting clauses in the Act of 1857 with regard to the position of the clergy of the Church of England, if the further grounds for divorce

above recommended be added. [Two key issues here were allowing Church of England clergy to refuse to conduct marriages for divorced persons with spouses still living and to withhold communion from divorced persons.] (*Report of the Royal Commission* 4, "Conspectus," 165.)

The minority—Ebor (Archbishop of York), Anson, and Dibdin—open their separate report with their disagreement respecting the extending of grounds beyond adultery. They too speak to principles, the testimony of witnesses, the rationale behind current ground of adultery, and each proposed new ground. In the end, they "recommend that . . . the law should not be altered so as to extend the grounds of divorce" (*Report of the Royal Commission* 4, "Minority Report," 189). They next take up the issue of providing greater facilities "to enable persons of slender means living at considerable distance from London to exercise their statutory rights under the Divorce Acts" (189). They agree with the majority that the High Court should sit locally, though they would allow this to happen in fewer sites across the nation. In addition they concur with the majority that all grounds, present or proposed, should be made equal between wives and husbands; that publicity should be curbed as recommended by the majority; and that the majority's recommendations on a range of issues relating to nullity and procedures relating to separation orders be adopted.

Over the years, the above recommendations were acted upon as follows.

APPENDIX I

Publicity

1911–1912: Sketching in court was voluntarily abandoned.
1926: The laws regulating the publicizing of divorce trials were modified. Any report other than a bona fide law report to be circulated among professionals could publish only the names, addresses, and occupations of the parties and witnesses; a concise statement of the charges, defenses, and countercharges of the proceedings; the court's decision thereon; submissions of any point of law and the decisions made thereon; the summing up of the judge and the finding of the jury if any; the observations of the judge.

Gender Equity

1923: Women were given equal access to divorce on the ground of adultery.

Cost and Jurisdiction

1914: An amendment in legal aid procedures allowed a few more cases to be brought to court by paupers. One could declare oneself a pauper if one's property (clothes and tools excluded) totaled fifty pounds or less, rather than the former twenty-five pounds or less. Changes in legal aid gradually made divorce more accessible to the poor (1918, 1920, 1926, and 1949), with the 1949 changes being the first to establish genuine access.
1967: Jurisdiction over divorce trials was extended be-

yond the Royal Courts of Justice in London. County courts could now hear undefended cases.

1973: A special procedure was introduced allowing certain divorce petitions to be processed by way of postal applications to the Divorce County Court.

1977: The above special procedure, allowing divorce "by mail" as some put it, was opened to all undefended cases.

Grounds

1937: Grounds for men and women were extended to include: three years' desertion; cruelty; prolonged and incurable insanity. A prohibition against seeking a divorce within the first three years of marriage was also enacted.

1956: A Report was issued by England's third *Royal Commission on Divorce and Matrimonial Causes*. Although the commissioners split nine to nine on the following recommendation, it became part of the English conversation on divorce: The concept of marital fault in divorce proceedings should be eliminated. The decree should be based on the concept of irremediable matrimonial breakdown. As some put it, the investigation should be less like a trial and more like an autopsy. The central questions become, is this marriage truly dead? What facts establish that finding?

1971: As the Divorce Reform Act of 1969 went into effect, irretrievable breakdown became England's ground for divorce. To establish such breakdown, parties could cite adultery; cruelty (with cruelty broadly defined to include "behavior" that one spouse finds intolerable); desertion for two years; two-year separation followed by a mutual consent to divorce; five-year separation followed by a desire to divorce on the part of one spouse.

APPENDIX I

The Entrance of Women
into Legal Processes

Although the issue of women gaining access to legal processes was not a formal recommendation of the commission, the concerns raised by many witnesses to the hearings were formally answered by the following act.

1919: The Sex Disqualification (Removal) Act stated that "a person should not be disqualified by sex or marriage from the exercise of any public function or from being appointed or holding any civil or judicial office or post or from entering or assuming or carrying on any civil profession or vocation" (quoted in Jane Lewis, *Women in England* 199). As Colin Rhys Lovell explains in *English Constitutional and Legal History,* the act meant that women could now be jurors, justices of the peace, solicitors, barristers, members of the House of Commons (the House of Lords delayed changing its regulations), judges on the bench of the High Court, and cabinet ministers.

As Davis and Murch, Smart, Eekelaar, and Maclean note, since the 1969 Divorce Reform Act, the main focus of reformist concern has shifted away from grounds toward what had been seen as ancillary issues: the fair division of property, the impact of divorce on children, and the economic consequences of divorce for women and children. (See Davis and Murch, *Grounds for Divorce;* Smart, *The Ties That Bind;* Eekelaar, *Regulating Divorce;* and Eekelaar and Maclean, *Maintenance After Divorce.*)

Surveys of Women's Attitudes
Toward Divorce

I. Survey Conducted by the Mothers'
Union, a Church of England Society

Mrs. Emelini Steinthal, appearing on June 7, 1910, presented to the Royal Commission on Divorce and Matrimonial Causes the Mothers' Union Survey in the form of two separate books of evidence. Book 1 records five questions and the responses of approximately forty-three officials of the Mothers' Union; respondents did not always answer every question. Mrs. Steinthal introduces Book 2 as being "exactly along the same lines" (*Report of the Royal Commission* 2:199): It asks four questions. Owing perhaps to a slightly altered format in the question and answer exchange at that point in her testimony or to a difference in the way the data were actually collected and recorded for Book 2, both the interrelationship of the questions in Books 1 and 2 and the exact nature of the responses to the questions in Book 2 are hard to discern.

Book 1

Question 1: Is there, so far as your experiences goes, a widespread or any demand for greater facilities for divorce amongst the poor?
No, 40; Yes, 1

Question 2: If the grounds of divorce were added to, e.g., if divorce were granted in cases of desertion, permanent lunacy, and long sentences of penal servitude, would it tend to lessen the sense of the binding character of the marriage tie amongst the poor?
Yes, would lessen, 36; No, would not lessen, 2

Question 3: Have you had personal experience in the working of separation orders granted by magistrates? If so, what is your experience as to the frequency of subsequent reconciliation? Subsequent reconciliation, greater proportion, 19; Not so many, 5

Question 4: What have you found to be the moral effect of separation orders—(a) In the case of husbands; (b) In the case of wives?
(a) Has a bad effect, 21; (b) Has a bad effect, 17
(a) Has a good effect, 0; (b) Has a good effect, 4

Question 5:
a. Does the publication of newspaper reports of divorce cases in your experience exercise a corrupting influence?
Response: Exercises a corrupting influence, 43; Does not exercise a corrupting influence, [no figure given]
b. Does the publicity now given to divorce cases act as a check upon immorality?
Response: Publicity does not act as a check, 40

Book 2

Question 1: Is there, as far as your experience goes, a widespread or any demand for greater facilities for divorce amongst—(a) The poor; (b) The lower middle classes.
Answer: (a) No, 72; Yes, 3 (b) No, 67; Yes, 5

Question 2: a. In what proportion of cases of applications for separation orders which have come under your notice has the application been withdrawn, or no order made, in consequence of a reconciliation having been effected between the parties?
Response: The majority are of opinion that the percentage of reconciliation is high. (2) That they come together either just before going into court or soon after. (3) One answers that she has known of reconciliation after a separation of twelve months. (4) If separation orders were delayed for three months they would seldom be needed. (5) That cases are often reconciled through the tact of a wise friend. The following percentages of reconciliations taking place are given: Llandaff, 50%; Tenbury, 99%; Ashton-under-Lyne, 70%; Newport, 75%; Ashton-under-Lyne 75% [this town is cited twice]; Hatfield, 50%; West Riding, 8 to 10%; Rochdale, 30%.

b. In what proportion of separation orders which have come under your notice has the order been superseded at the instance of the parties, a reconciliation having been effected?
Response: Percentages of reconciliation: Stepney, 50%; Ashton-under-Lyne, 2%; Rochdale 50%; Keighley, 75%; Bradford, 50%; Tenby, 90%; Newport, 30%; Hatfield, 35%; Chester, 50%; Lyne, 30%.

c. What in your experience have been the chief causes leading up to applications for separation orders?
Response: [The number of officials citing a particular cause is given first, followed by the cause.] 7, desertion; 22, cruelty; 46, drink; 5, immorality; 11, early marriage; 4, neglect; 6, incompatibility; 1, extravagance; 3, idleness; 1, dirt; 6, temper; 1, want of self-control; 1, clubs; 1, interference by mother-in-law; 2, ignorance of duties; 2, unemployment; 1, gambling; 1, laxity of moral training.

Question 3: Does the publicity of newspaper reports of divorce cases, in your experience, exercise a corrupt influence? Does the publicity now given to divorce cases act as a check upon immorality?
a. Exercises corrupt influence, 57; Does not exercise corrupt influence in any case, [no figure given]
b. Publicity does not act as a check, 50; Publicity necessary, but details pernicious, and only name and verdict published, 13

Question 4: If divorce were made cheap, and were allowed in mere cases of desertion, would the result, in your opinion, tend generally to the promotion of morality amongst (a) the poor, (b) the lower middle classes, or in an opposite direction?
a. That divorce (cheaper) would not tend for morality, 44
That divorce (cheaper) would tend for morality, 3
Doubtful, 1
(b) Lower middle class—opposite direction, 1
(*Report of the Royal Commission* 2:199–203.)

II. Survey Conducted by the Women's Cooperative Guild

Appearing on November 9, 1910, Margaret Llewelyn Davies presented to the Royal Commission the Women's Co-operative Guild's survey, conducted in association with distributive industrial cooperative societies. The guild's survey also had two components, the first comprised two questions sent out to 431 branches, representing 23,501 members. The second comprised

SURVEYS OF WOMEN'S ATTITUDES

seven questions, including the two asked of the branches. It was sent out to 124 elected officials of the guild. In addition to the data she presented on each question, Davies included many supporting case stories.

Question 1: Should the present grounds for divorce be the same for men and women?
Branch replies: 413 out of 431 with 22,558 members, yes (including 25 branches with 1,438 members who are opposed to divorce).
Three branches with 156 members, no.
Twelve branches with 650 members do not reply.
[Three are unaccounted for.]
124 women: 123 yes, including 13 who are opposed to divorce. One does not reply.

Question 2: Should divorce proceedings be cheapened, and where necessary be free of all cost?
a. Should divorce proceedings be cheaper?
Branch replies: 364 branches with 19,124 members, yes, including 6 branches with 223 members opposed to divorce.
53 branches with 3,000 odd members, no. Of these, 33 branches have 2,064 members opposed divorce.
14 branches with 1,155 members are doubtful or make no response.
124 women: 119, yes (including nine who are opposed to divorce); 3, no; 1—only cheaper in exceptional cases; 2 make no response.
b. Should all costs of Divorce proceedings be paid by the State where necessary?
No branch responses.
97 women out of 124, yes, of whom 6 are opposed to or doubtful about divorce; 6 no, of whom 3 are opposed to or doubtful about divorce; 4 doubtful; 17 no response.

Question 3: Should there be additional grounds for divorce?

a. Should the husband's refusal to maintain wife and family be a ground for divorce?

91 women, yes, of whom 3 are not in favor of divorce; 12 no, of whom 3 are opposed to divorce; 2 are in favor of punishment or separation as a preliminary step; 6 are doubtful, 1 being opposed to divorce; 13 no response.

b. Should insanity be a ground for divorce?

98 out of 124 yes, 4 of whom are opposed to divorce and 18 saying only incurable insanity should be grounds for divorce; 14 no, 4 being opposed to divorce; 2 are doubtful, 1 of whom is opposed to divorce; 10 no response.

c. Should desertion for a period of 2 years be a ground for divorce?

88 women, yes, 4 of whom are opposed to divorce. Within that, 7 would make the period of desertion from 3 to 5 years; 1 would make the period of desertion from 8 to 10 years; 7 no, 3 of whom are opposed to divorce; 7 doubtful, 2 of whom are opposed divorce; 14 no response.

d. Should cruelty be a ground for divorce?

100 women, yes, 4 of whom are opposed to divorce; 2 no, 1 of whom is opposed to divorce; 5 doubtful, 2 of whom are opposed to divorce; 17 no response.

e. Should drunkenness be a ground for divorce? (sent to only 40 individuals).

26 women, yes, 1 of whom is opposed to divorce; 5 no, including 1 who would allow separation, 3 of whom are opposed to divorce; 2 are doubtful; 7 no response.

A few others who were not asked the question suggested it as a cause.

f. Should imprisonment be a ground for divorce?

This question was not asked, but a few suggested that it should be.

g. Should a separation order which has lasted for three years be a ground for divorce?

75 women, yes, 3 of whom are opposed to divorce; 7, no, 3 of whom are opposed to divorce; 7 doubtful; 35 no response.

h. Should mutual consent be a ground for divorce?

82 women, yes, 2 of whom are opposed to divorce; 12, no, 5 of whom are opposed to divorce; 15 doubtful, 2 of whom are opposed to divorce; 15 no response.

i. Should serious incompatibility be a cause for divorce?

75 women, yes, of whom 2 are opposed to divorce; 10, no, 2 of whom are opposed to divorce; 7 doubtful, 1 of whom is opposed to divorce; 32, no response.

Question 4: Should divorce be allowed when both parties are guilty?

86 women, yes, 4 of whom are opposed to divorce; 12, no, of whom 5 are opposed to divorce; 8, doubtful; 24, no response.

Question 5: Should the guardianship of children be given to the parent most fit on general grounds?

73 women, yes, with the following breakdown: 49 say yes, 3 of whom are opposed to divorce; 24 consider the mother should be guardian unless irretrievably bad, and 3 of these are opposed to divorce; 7, no, 2 of whom are opposed to divorce; 2, doubtful; 29, no response.

Question 6: Should the maintenance allowance and alimony under separation orders and divorce be collected by the court?

101, yes; 4, no; 19, no response.

Question 7: Administration of the Law.

a. Where should divorces cases be tried?

76 women favor county courts; 10 favor special local courts; 3 favor assize courts; 4 favor local courts, but not police courts; 3 opposed local courts; 2 opposed to local courts unless cases tried with closed doors; 27 no response.
b. Should women serve on juries? [This question was also asked of branches.]
104 women, yes; 4, no; 3, doubtful; 13, no response.
Branch replies: 311 branches with 17,991 members, yes; 84 branches with 3,390 members, no; 36 branches with 2,120 members are undecided or do not reply.

[Davies comments that several women who said no to serving on juries were concerned about cost, citing "the hardship of men being compelled to sit at the assizes and bear all their own expenses" (*Report of the Royal Commission* 3: 160).]

Opinions without data were also given on the value of mediation and the necessity of curbing publicity. (*Report of the Royal Commission* 3: 152–161)

Introduction

1 See especially Chapter VI, "The Trouble with Women."

2 Donald Read, for example, introduces *Edwardian England* with an astute discussion of a range of divisive issues but ignores the debate over of divorce. See too J. B. Priestley, *The Edwardians*; Colin Cross, *The Liberals in Power*; R. J. Minney, *The Edwardian Age*; Alan O'Day, ed., *The Edwardian Age*; and Paul Thompson, *The Edwardians. Feminism and the Family in England 1880–1939* by Carol Dyhouse and "The Family and the Role of Women" by Suzann Buckley analyze Edwardian debates over family issues but, again, minimally treat the topic of divorce.

3 For comparative data, see Lawrence Stone, *Road to Divorce* (416–418).

4 The following current works convey this sense of search: *In the Child's Best Interests?* by Christopher Clulow and Christopher Vincent; *Wedlocked?* by David Clark and Douglas Haldane; *Perfect Partners?* by Bob Mullan; *In Search of a Policy* by Joan C. Brown; and *Lost Hearts: Talking about Divorce* by Danny Danziger.

5 Hynes writes that for many the debate was considered to be England's last holy war (209).

6 *Marriage, Divorce, and Morality* (37).

7 Christina Sinclair Bremner, Preface, *Divorce and Morality*, 7.

8 Reissman, *Divorce Talk: Women and Men Make Sense of Personal Relationships*; Danziger, *Lost Hearts: Talking about Divorce*; Davis and Murch, *Grounds for Divorce*.

9 See Davis and Murch, *Grounds for Divorce* (14–18, 93).

10 Haskey, "The Proportion of Marriages Ending in Divorce," 4. The revised estimate is found in John Eekelaar, *Regulating Divorce* (54). Eekelaar cites the 1990 predictions of Kiernan and Wicks.

11 Stone himself slips into this assumption when he writes that before 1918 "divorce was still largely out of the reach

or even the imagination of the poor" (387). I argue that divorce was very imaginable by the poor, before and after 1918.

12 In *Divorce Talk*, Reissman does a careful narrative analysis of the stories of 104 recently separated or divorced men and women in the Northeastern region of the United States during the 1980s. Danziger's *Lost Hearts* is an anthology of personal accounts drawn from his interviews with divorced British men and women. In "No-Fault Divorce Films: Hollywood's Changing Morality," Deegan looks at shifts in Hollywood's depiction of divorce, especially at no-fault scenarios in films such as "Falling in Love" (1984) and "Twice in a Lifetime" (1985). Eekelaar's *Regulating Divorce* takes its starting point from interviews with thirty-eight registrars in England and pursues questions about the ideology and visions that inform the practice of family law. In *The Ties That Bind,* Smart pursues parallel questions. Drawing on the perceptions of a range of officials engaged in the practice of family law, she argues eloquently for a feminist analysis of marriage and divorce that will combat the current division of labor that makes women and children so vulnerable to poverty. Glendon's *Abortion and Divorce in Western Law* is a comparative study of the legal systems in six Western nations and of the kind of story each of those systems conveys to its citizens on the issues of divorce and abortion. And Berenson's *The Trial of Madame Caillaux,* employing a thick description of the famous murder trial of Madame Caillaux in France on the eve of World War I, offers, in its fourth chapter, an analysis of the way the respective divorces of each of the two principals in that trial were represented by the prosecution and the defense.

13 Sir Gorell Barnes became president of the Probate, Divorce, and Admirality Division of the High Courts of Justice in February, 1905. In February, 1909, he resigned the post (the Hon. Mr. Justice Bigham succeeded him) and became, in the same month, Lord Gorell, Baron of the United Kingdom. Later in that same year, he was named

as Chairman of the Royal Commission on Divorce and Matrimonial Causes.

14 Information on the Dodd case is available in the divorce records at the Public Records Office, Chancery Lane, London, as well as in *The Annual Digest of the Times Law Reports* 22 (1905–1906): 484–491.

15 *Report of the Royal Commission on Divorce and Matrimonial Causes* 4:9.

16 In English divorce practice, a successful petitioner is granted two decrees. The first, the *decree nisi* or "decree unless," is provisional for a specified period of time. If, during that period, no circumstances occur or are discovered that would block the divorce, a second decree, the *decree absolute,* is awarded. During the Edwardian era, the probationary period was six months. As of 1992, the period is six weeks. See Fiona Shakleton and Olivia Timbs, *The Divorce Handbook.*

17 See Mary Lyndon Shanley, *Feminism, Marriage, and the Law in Victorian England* (131– 155). The emphasis on the welfare of children was reiterated with respect to divorce cases in Stark *v.* Stark, 1910 (Eekelaar, *Regulating Divorce,* 42).

18 Burgoyne, *Divorce Matters,* 76.

19 See Eekelaar, *Regulating Divorce,* 42. The case of Anna Northover, discussed in Chapter 1, indicates the kinds of exceptions that were made. For analyses of current custody issues in Western Europe, North America, and Australia, see Carol Smart and Selma Sevenhuijsen, *Child Custody and the Politics of Gender.*

20 The 80 percent figure for England's working class is given by Read, *Edwardian England* (31); Paul Thompson, *The Edwardians* (17); and Edgar Royston Pike, *Human Documents of the Lloyd George Era* (20).

21 Maud Pember Reeves's *Round About a Pound a Week* gives a dramatic indication of what a bill of between forty to sixty pounds would have meant to a working-class family. Struggling hard on approximately fifty-two pounds a year, the families she analyzed—who were, as she says, by

no means England's poorest—could never have saved up enough. For a further sense of what a pound was worth during this decade, see Thompson's *The Edwardians*; Pike's *Human Documents of the Lloyd George Era*; and Carol Adam's *Ordinary Lives a Hundred Years Ago*.

22 A. C. Plowden, a well-known metropolitan police court magistrate from London, strongly disagreed with Gorell Barnes's characterization of magistrates. He felt that magistrates were the best possible officials to deal with marital breakdown. See his autobiography, *Grain or Chaff?* (243) and his testimony before the Royal Commission (*Report of the Royal Commission* 2: 273).

23 Dodd *v.* Dodd, *Annual Digest of The Times Law Reports* 22: 491.

24 For example, under circumstances similar to the Dodd case, in both Levy *v.* Levy (1904) and Smith *v.* Smith (1905), the court had found for the wife (*Annual Digest of the Times Law Reports* 21:157–158; and 22:249).

25 The data indicate that approximately 80 percent of Edwardians who got to court received their decrees. Data for 1906 show that within that figure, 88 percent of the wives who petitioned for a divorce received one. For husbands the figure was 82 percent. In 1909, the figures are 90 percent for wives, 84 percent for husbands. These figures are typical for the decade. See *Report of the Royal Commission* 4, appendix 3:28.

26 DeMontmorency, *John Gorell Barnes*, 164–166, 173.

27 Hynes gives more credit to Lord Russell for initiating the debate than does Haynes (*The Edwardian Turn of Mind*, 192).

28 Haynes, "Introduction," *Divorce Problems of Today*, v.

29 Several societies devoted to divorce law reform had been organized, including "The Society for Promoting Reforms in the Marriage and Divorce Laws of England" in 1903 and "The Divorce Law Reform Association" formed soon after (Hynes, *The Edwardian Turn of Mind*, 192). These banded together in 1906 under the name of "The United Divorce Law Reform Union." Presidents included

W. G. Ramsay Fairfax, Arthur Conan Doyle, and Richard T. Gates.

30 Haynes, "The Late Lord Gorell and Divorce Law Reform," in *Divorce as It Might Be,* 63–65.

31 Bremner, *Divorce and Morality,* 17. Bremner's point is attested to by the sheer quantity of books and articles published on the topic. For a partial listing, see nonfiction primary sources in the Bibliography. Anticipating studies written late in the decade is a highly thoughtful work, *The Question of English Divorce: An Essay.* That it came out anonymously in 1903 reinforces Haynes's sense of an initial taboo on the topic. Of England's numerous newspapers, *The Daily Telegraph* is praised for its early coverage of the debate (see Haynes, "Introduction," *Divorce Problems of Today,* v).

32 Chapman, *Marriage and Divorce,* 131–138.

33 See Shanley, *Feminism, Marriage, and the Law,* 74.

34 Lee Holcombe, *Wives and Property,* 203.

35 More significant would have been legislation that recognized the wife's right to financial compensation for her housewifely services, either through a governmental payment or a legal right to a portion of her husband's wage (or property, e.g., the marital home). Both were continually discussed during this time. See for example the debate between H. G. Wells and Dora Marsden in *The Freewoman* (February 29–March 21, 1912) and also Burgoyne, *Divorce Matters,* 59–70.

36 *Women, Work, and Family,* 196–197. See too Jane Lewis, *Women in England,* 149.

37 Folbre, "The Unproductive Housewife," 463–464. Folbre is working with a range of census data. See also Diana Gittins on the specific failure of the census to take into account seasonal or part time work (*Fair Sex,* 95).

38 See Clementina Black's superb collection of Edwardian studies on married women's work. The very purpose of Black's study was to gather information. Nor was it easy. As the chapter on Newcastle by Annie Abram reports, many married women successfully hid their waged

labors. For a review of scholarship on this issue, see Janice H. Harris, "Feminist Representations of Wives and Work."

39 Eekelaar offers a thorough-going critique of Allan Bloom's attempt to link particular historical changes in people's perceptions of family dynamics with changes of attitude that go back to the Enlightenment, for example "the rise in individualism" (*Regulating Divorce*, 16–19).

40 Hynes is especially helpful in his discussion of these issues.

41 In *Divorce and Morality*, Bremner sees Germany's laws as a potential spur to England: "The fear of Germany, the jealousy of a physique, taking all classes together, far superior to our own, a fact that the Kaiser has emphasized on several occasions, may yet prove the beginning of wisdom and accelerate the course of legislation in the direction of equality [of grounds between men and women]" (62). Haynes puts it more generally. "In its essential principles the German law is in line with that of most civilized countries, while our law is not" ("Our Divorce Law," *Divorce Problems of Today*, 45).

42 See Shanley, *Feminism, Marriage, and the Law*, chapter 1, for a feminist analysis of the Divorce Act of 1857.

43 Gail Savage, "Divorce and the Law in England and France Prior to the First World War," 502, 505.

44 As reported in the *Evening Standard and St. James Gazette*, the Registrar-General's data for 1907 showed 918,042 births, of which 881,853 were legitimate, and 36,189 were illegitimate. Thus, approximately one child in twenty-five born in 1907 was considered illegitimate.

45 In Manchester, writes Dyhouse, 8,000 out of 11,000 volunteers had to be rejected as physically unfit. See "Good Wives and Little Mothers" (22). Conscription had thrown a spotlight on England's high rate of infant mortality as well. During the following decade, cultural anxiety over infant well-being is demonstrated by a series of parliamentary acts and the regular gathering of data. Such anxiety paid off. Infant mortality rates dropped during the Ed-

wardian decade and continued to do so through the war and into the 1920s and 1930s (Jane Lewis, *The Politics of Motherhood*, 15–16).

46 *Divorce and Morality*, 61–62. Phillips gives an overview of European eugenic interest in divorce (507–513). See also Hynes, *The Edwardian Turn of Mind*, chapter 2. Edwardian eugenicists who were particularly engaged in the issue included Montague Crackanthorpe, C. W. Saleeby, and Christina Bremner. As president of the Eugenics Education Society, Crackanthorpe, along with two medical colleagues, testified before the Royal Commission on Divorce (*Report of the Royal Commission* 3:84–101).

47 *Report of the Royal Commission* 4, appendix 3: 32. Comparing the remedy for marital failure represented by a separation order versus a divorce is a concern here and in Chapter 2. Given my focus on divorce, however, I have not treated the intricacies of separation law nor the debate over its reform. A detailed review of standing Edwardian law on separations and recommendations for change are found in the *Report of the Royal Commission* 4, pts. 12 and 13:66–82.

48 Armstrong, *Desire and Domestic Fiction*, 169–174.

49 Holmes, "The New Licensing Bill," 515.

50 Eekelaar and Maclean, *Maintenance after Divorce*, 2.

51 In *The Evolution of National Insurance in Great Britain*, Bentley B. Gilbert indicates the extent to which Lloyd George turned to Germany for guidance in setting up his social reforms (291–293).

52 See Harris, "Feminist Representations of Wives and Work"; "Challenging the Script of the Heterosexual Couple"; and "Wifely Speech and Silence."

53 Smart, *The Ties That Bind*, xiii.

54 *The Ties That Bind*, 17–23. In "Locating Law," Brophy and Smart provide a good historical overview of feminist disagreements regarding engagement in legal reform.

55 Anne Bottomley, "What Is Happening to Family Law?"

56 Lenore Weitzman, *The Divorce Revolution*, xi, 31–36. In

arguing that the move to no-fault grounds did indeed harm women, Weitzman also reviews the arguments mounted by feminists in favor of no-fault divorce.

57 Brophy, "Custody Law," 57.

58 As Dyhouse explains, "feminists who focused their activities narrowly on the pursuit of the Suffrage tended to avoid embroiling their cause with other, controversial issues of sexual morality. This was sometimes seen as deliberate political strategy" (*Feminism and the Family*, 174–175). Ray Strachey reinforces Dyhouse's view, noting Millicent Garrett Fawcett's reluctance to speak out on any issue not directly related to suffrage. Testifying, as she did, to the Royal Commission on Divorce and Matrimonial Causes was thus a rare exception for her (Strachey, *Fawcett*, 224–225). Not surprisingly, as I indicate in Chapter 2, Fawcett tried to steer clear of the highly divisive issue of broadening grounds and insisted that she be considered simply an individual witness, representing no organization or society. Two eloquent exceptions to this tendency among the Edwardian suffragists are Margaret Nevinson and Ada Nield Chew. Both consistently embed their pro-suffrage arguments in scenes of domestic strife, including scenes of anger and/or despair over England's restrictive divorce laws. See Nevinson's short stories in *The Spoilt Child of the Law* and Chew's tales in *The Life and Writings of Ada Nield Chew*. For additional references to Chew's stories, see Ardis's entry on Chew in *The Dictionary of Literary Biography*.

59 See for example the differing stances taken by Edwardian feminists testifying to the Royal Commission: Millicent Garrett Fawcett, vol. 2: 371–379; Helena Maria Swanwick, vol. 2: 459–468; Dr. Ethel Bentham, vol. 3: 30–38; and Margaret Llewelyn Davies, vol. 3: 149–171. Swanwick later wrote of her discomfort at disagreeing with Lady Frances Balfour who was serving as one of the commissioners (*I Have Been Young*, 211). One notes also the lack of agreement between the two feminist commissioners, Lady Balfour and May Tennant.

60 Delgado, "Storytelling for Oppositionists and Others."
61 *Regulating Divorce,* 6.

Chapter 1 Stock Stories

1 See the testimony of Mr. A. G. Jeans, *Report of the Royal Commission* 3: 186.
2 Interruptions in the semiotic system are in fact scattered around the building, but scarcely so as to be visible to the petitioner. For example, if one approaches the Royal Courts by way of the professionals' entrance on the north side, one passes under a statue of Moses, a legislator whose presumably lax views on divorce and remarriage problematized the Church of England line. Mounted above the portal used by the judges is a comical carving of a dog and cat. If one comes back inside, one notices the odd gap that architect George Street left in one of the colonnades. Historians of the building suggest that Street's wrangling cat and dog were meant to indicate a human tendency to quarrel, his gap a reminder of human imperfection. Only Jesus Christ, declared the religious Street, could create a perfect building. All is not unified, dignified, or symmetrical here. (For background on Street and on the building, see *The Royal Courts of Justice: An Introduction for Visitors,* 5; and *Royal Courts of Justice: An Illustrated Guide,* 40.)
3 As they reflect literacy rates in England, Masterman's figures should perhaps be taken with caution. Richard D. Altick explains that the 97 percent figure for literacy in England in 1900 represents "only those young men and women, who, upon being married in that year, were able to sign their names" ("The Reading Public in England and America in 1900," in *Writers, Readers, and Occasions,* 212). At the same time, argues Alan J. Lee, if one looks at a variety of indicators, one can posit genuine widespread

reading ability by the turn of the century (*The Origins of the Popular Press*, 32–33).

4 The top four metropolitan Sunday papers in terms of circulation were *Reynold's News, News of the World, Lloyd's Weekly News*, and *Observer, Weekly Dispatch*. The estimated total circulation for all four combined was 6,525,000 per week (Lee, *Origins of the Popular Press*, 293).

5 Q. D. Leavis adds to Bell's description: "*News of the World* is read on the doorstep or in bed" (*Fiction and the Reading Public*, 3). The Sunday papers were political in origin, being initiated in the 1820s and 1830s as radical working-class publications. They grew steadily less radical after 1850 (Lee, *Origins of the Popular Press*, 71, 218).

6 Selecting which of the trials will receive longer treatment seems based as much on the human interest of the story as on the prominence of the parties concerned, though theatrical figures typically receive fairly full coverage. Thus the divorce of well-known publisher William Heinemann receives one-fourth the coverage received by the presumably more intriguing divorce of Mrs. Edith Arnold by Mr. Edward Henry Arnold, clerk in a furniture store, in *News of the World*, January 22, 1905. The Heinemann report gives the reader a glimpse into the lavish carryings-on of the faithless Mrs. Heinemann, but does not elaborate. The Arnold tale leads off the page with a triple headline—TELL TALE DIARY/BOY CORRESPONDENT IN DIVORCE SUIT/THE INFATUATION OF A FULHAM MAN'S WIFE—and gives a detailed account of Mrs. Arnold's shocking affair with a young lad who had been something of a friend of the family. The story includes quotations from numerous love letters and excerpts from the boy's impassioned diary (6).

7 See the Introduction for background on Edwardian custody laws.

8 See Brake, "The Old Journalism and the New," in Wiener, *Papers for the Millions* (1–2) and Lee, *Origins of the Popular Press* (120–130) for analyses of the new journalism's form and content. Altick argues that the sensational-

ist bent within new journalism reached a new plateau in 1861 with the reporting of two extraordinary crimes (*Deadly Encounters*).

9 See for example discussions of the Stirling trial in the *Report of the Royal Commission* 3: 186, 202. As the witnesses make clear, coverage of this particular trial was extraordinary. Yet, like current coverage of infamous trials, the Stirling report represented a general tendency respecting the freedom of the media. The Northover story would be a more typical "long" report—detailed and extended but contained within a single edition of the paper.

10 In Scotland a husband's adultery, without additional acts, was grounds for divorce.

11 This summary is drawn from *News of the World,* January 24, 1909: 9.

12 Studies of Edwardian fashion indicate that the costumes of Mabel Atherton and Clara Stirling were exquisitely in vogue. From their hats to their gowns and stoles, they were walking fashion plates. The "Merry Widow" hat worn by Mrs. Stirling had become fashionable in 1907. It is described by Douglas Russell as an "excessively large" affair, named after the heroine in the Lehar operetta. Mabel's equally fashionable toque, trimmed with the feather of the endangered egret, was a soft turbanlike construction (Russell, *Costume History and Style,* 398). The two elaborately dressed women, and the reporters' attentiveness to their costumes, raise complex questions about how to interpret their (and our own) self-display. Jennifer Craik, in *The Face of Fashion,* problematizes the standard argument, to wit, that female costume is solely a function of patriarchal pride and desire for control. According to this argument, the well-dressed female body is an object that the male has constrained in its physical movement (in Edwardian fashion by the corset) and decorated with the signs of his wealth. Contending that this view denies the multifaceted nature of male/female power relations, Craik would have us expand our understanding of how fashion

works so as to include notions of female pleasure and power, as well as an understanding of the range of "learnings, orientations, identifications, and sexual knowledges" women and men express through fashion (47). For two photographic surveys documenting Edwardian fashion, see Katrina Rolley and Caroline Aish, *Fashion in Photographs 1900–1920* and Alison Gernsheim, *Victorian and Edwardian Fashion*.

13 The March 11, 1909, report in *The London Times* closes with an indication that Clara Stirling and Lord Northland intended to file an appeal. Papers on the Stirling trial at the Scottish Record Office in Edinburgh show that an initial appeal was filed at the conclusion of the trial, on March 10, 1909, but then withdrawn two months later on May 12, 1909. The parties continued to dispute court costs as late as the following January.

14 For an introduction to this debate, see Catharine A. MacKinnon, "Feminism, Marxism, Method, and the State: Toward Feminist Jurisprudence"; Toni Massaro, "Empathy, Legal Storytelling, and the Rule of Law"; Kim Lane Schepple, "Foreword: Telling Stories"; and Ann Scales, "The Emergence of Feminist Jurisprudence."

15 Quoted in Haynes, "The Publicity of Divorce," *Divorce Problems of Today*, 144.

16 Bennett and Feldman are quick to point out that the use of competing narratives in courts of law is culture specific. Guilt or innocence can be determined by different means, for example, by physical ordeal, the taking of an oath, or the submitting of more or less apt proverbs (27).

17 Geertz, "Local Knowledge: Fact and Law in Comparative Perspective," *Local Knowledge*, 173–175. While coming at the issues from different perspectives, James Boyd White, Robert M. Cover, Ronald Dworkin, and Kim Lane Schepple have all contributed to the analysis of law as a narrative activity, a branch of rhetoric. See also Stanley Fish, "Working on the Chain Gang" for a reaction to Dworkin. For a collection of exemplary essays on storytelling and the law, see *Michigan Law Review* 87 (1989).

In "Trusting the Tale," Martin Kreiswirth offers an overview of the explosion of interest in narrative across the disciplines in the 1980s.

18 Edwardian analyses of this distinction between the adultery of a wife and husband employ the following rationales. First, males are naturally more promiscuous and sexually active; thus, their acts of adultery do not signify any real shift of love or affection away from their wives. Second, women are more forgiving than men; men are more jealous. For good or ill, men feel they own and must guard and protect their wife's body from other males. Third, when wives commit adultery, they run the risk of burdening their legal husbands with another man's child. Depending on his choice of partner, married or unmarried, adultery on the part of a husband may or may not so burden his married brothers. The "confusion of progeny" argument is continually debated during the Royal Commission hearings. Many Edwardians saw the illogic of blaming adulterous wives for getting pregnant while absolving adulterous husbands for getting other women pregnant, be those other women wives or not. See Burgoyne, *Divorce Matters,* for a good history of the "confusion of progeny" concept and the political interests it served (44–45).

Chapter 2 Counterstories

1 Delgado describes outgroups as "groups whose marginality defines the boundaries of the mainstream, whose voice and perspective—whose consciousness—has been suppressed, devalued, and abnormalized" (2412).

2 As indicated in the Introduction, the commission also wrestled with a series of changes in the Separation Acts. See *Report of the Royal Commission* 4, pts. 12 and 13:66–82, and my Appendix I.

3 Brooks, *Reading for the Plot,* 8–9, 234–235.

4 Balfour, *Ne Obliviscaris,* 423. Hynes records a similar account of King Edward's reluctance to have women serve on the commission (186), as indeed does Lord Gorell's son Ronald in his introduction to DeMontmorency's biography (12). Clearly the story was bruited about.

5 Violet Markham, *May Tennant,* 43.

6 West, "The Divorce Commission," 124–127.

7 Helena Maria Lucy Swanwick, testifying as editor of "The Common Cause" and colleague of May Tennant, echoes Balfour's affection for Lord Guthrie. When Sir Frederick Treves and Sir William Anson "tried to put [her] out, Lord Gorell and Lord Guthrie were perfectly splendid" (*I Have Been Young,* 211). Swanwick's feminist interests were strong and varied. See Swanwick, *The Future of the Woman's Movement.*

8 "Divorce Report," *The Saturday Review* (November 16, 1912): 602.

9 Roe, "Applied Narrative Analysis," 563.

10 A selection of both the resolutions and the letters was published in vol. 4 of the *Report of the Royal Commission* as appendices 25 and 26.

11 As did other witnesses (for example Davies), Chapman published a book based on his testimony. See Chapman, *Marriage and Divorce,* and Davies, *Working Women and Divorce.* At the time, the phrase "working women" denoted class rather than occupation outside the home.

12 Adultery that took place within the family home could legally be considered as cruel. Thus, Chapman's plaintiff, if she had funds, could probably have won a case for divorce.

13 The strategy of ceasing their narratives with either no real closure or a scandalous one is adopted by many of the witnesses with counterstories, with Dr. Ethel Bentham and Dr. Harold Scurfield being among the most eloquent. Scurfield's testimony is recorded in vol. 2: 379–393; Bentham's in vol. 3: 30–38. After Scurfield relates a complicated tale of husbands, wives, children, and lovers all living together under the same roof, the conservative Sir

Lewis Dibdin barks, Why do you tell us these "repulsive" stories? In order, Scurfield replies, to show the disregard for the marriage bond that prevails under England's current bad laws (*Report* 2:386–387).

14 Some Anglican women clearly felt pressured to sign the petition. As one wrote, "I have just resigned from the Mothers' Union, of which I have been a member for 15 years, because I do not hold with the line they are taking over this divorce. I am told that they are getting up a petition, and that people are signing it *just to please the ladies,* although as a matter of fact they approve of divorce" (*Report* 3:151).

15 Plowden's name appears often in the Edwardian press as a featured speaker at this or that club or gathering. His autobiography, *Grain or Chaff?,* is highly readable and often cited by social historians of this era.

16 Anticipating a call to give testimony during the spring 1910 sittings, the guild had conducted an early survey, drawing on only forty participants, a number closely in line with the Mothers' Union survey. Having the summer months allowed the guild to add one further question to their survey and to contact eighty-four additional members. By the fall, they had an impressive pool of 124 lengthy responses from individuals, in addition to their separate survey of the branches.

17 There are occasional insignificant differences in the wording of a particular survey question as it is first read out by Davies during the hearings and then entered into the minutes of evidence in the form of her survey books. Thus, my quotations from her testimony contain occasional minor discrepancies when compared to the survey books summarized in Appendix II.

18 For studies of domestic violence within the Victorian and Edwardian periods see Ellen Ross, " 'Fierce Questions and Taunts' "; Shanley, *Feminism, Marriage, and the Law,* chapter 6; and A. James Hammerton, *Cruelty and Companionship.*

19 Eekelaar, *Regulating Divorce,* 23, 42.

20 *Gender Justice,* 29–33.

21 Given Millicent Garrett Fawcett's many and powerful or-
ganizational connections, her decision to speak strictly as
an individual—and not as a participant in a network of
women—is noteworthy. One can speculate that she felt it
important to testify but that she wished to avoid fac-
tionalizing her suffrage colleagues. Thus she speaks for
herself. Thus too she refuses to enter the contentious debate over extending grounds and focuses instead on issues
strictly related to male and female equity before the law—
or tries to (*Report* 2: 371–379).

22 "Representation," 21.

23 Bottomley, "What Is Happening to Family Law," 184.

24 "Workshop," 121. *Women's Rights Law Reporter* 10 (1988):
107–141.

25 See Dale Bauer, *Feminist Dialogics*, for a fine demonstra-
tion of the ways in which theory on interpretive communities is enhanced by an analysis of gender.

26 Equally disappointing to Lord Gorell was the *Times'* decision to publish the Minority Report in its entirety and
circulate it for free as a supplement to the paper ("Introduction," DeMontmorency, *John Gorrell Barnes*, 16–17).

27 Ibid., 181–188.

28 See Barnes, "Divorce Law and Its Reform," *The Contemporary Review* 103 (1913): 62–69.

29 It was precisely the ability to generate and record a national conversation on divorce; to recognize the plurality
of views expressed; and to respond with a policy that captured the conversation, in its agreements and disagreements, that Mary Ann Glendon praises in looking at the
French divorce law reform of 1979. The Edwardian Parliament's incapacity to use the Royal Commission report
to write a set of interrelated reforms that corresponded
with the national conversation is, in her view, not surprising however and relates to a general approach to legal reform characteristic of the American and English systems.
See Glendon, *Abortion and Divorce,* chapter 3.

Chapter 3 Stock Stories versus Counterstories

1 For most critics of Edwardian fiction, this subgenre has been invisible. See, for example, Jefferson Hunter's *Edwardian Fiction* and John Batchelor's *The Edwardian Novelists*. Hynes and Jane Eldridge Miller are exceptions. Hynes analyzes Bennett's *Whom God Hath Joined,* and Miller, devoting a chapter to the Edwardian marriage novel, gives brief attention to the theme. My titles were drawn from contemporary book reviews in the *Times Literary Supplement* and *The Spectator*; Ernest A. Baker, *A Guide to the Best Fiction in English: 1913*; Diva Daims and Janet Grimes, eds., *Toward a Feminist Tradition*; Donald K. Hartman, *Themes and Settings in Fiction*; Edward S. Lauterbach and W. Eugene Davis, *The Transitional Age: British Literature*; and Samuel J. Rogal, *A Chronological Outline of British Literature*. In the main, I limited my search to novels that actually move their characters into the legal system to consult with lawyers, learn about the law, and either go to trial or prepare to do so. (An important plot device shows characters balked or withdrawing their petitions.) Because a full-scale bibliographic survey was beyond the intent of this chapter, I offer my thirty-six titles as a reliable sample rather than complete listing. A review of the publication dates shows a bulge between 1910 and 1914, suggesting that the authors of these fictions were responding to the interest in divorce generated by the hearings of the Royal Commission. A preponderance of the novels selected turned out to have been written by women (twenty-six by women, eleven by men). However, divorce novels that fall just outside my time period show strong representation by male writers (from Henry James's *What Maisie Knew* [1897] to Morley Roberts's *Hearts of Women* [1919], Galsworthy's *In Chancery* [1920], William Babington Maxwell's *Remedy Against Sin* [1920], and a bit later Alec Waugh's *Nor Many Waters* [1928] and A. P. Herbert's *Holy Deadlock* [1934]). Thus, I have not wanted to argue that

divorce was a topic with which women novelists necessarily identified more readily than did men. Equally important, as this chapter shows, in the series of debates
enacted *among* the divorce novels, male and female authors
situate themselves with equal frequency across the camps.
As indicated in Chapter 2, it matters greatly that women
are participating in the Edwardian exchange of narratives
on divorce, but in stance and style the women demonstrate a rich diversity.

2 Ann Ardis provides a valuable analysis of these late nineteenth century innovations, looking in particular at the
significance of the new format for publishers, the writers
who signed on with them, and readers (38–41).

3 Bennett, *How to Become an Author,* 189.

4 In characterizing the authors of divorce novels as professionals who were tapping into a topical issue, I distinguish
them from the authors of the New Woman novels of the
decade before, many of whom—especially the women—
were new to the profession and treated with a good deal of
critical skepticism (Ardis, *New Women, New Novels,* 38–
50).

5 Wells, quoted in Hunter, *Edwardian Fiction* (47). See too
Bennett, *How to Become an Author* (24–25).

6 Lee, *Origins of the Popular Press,* 293.

7 "Aimed" and "designed" are key words here. One encounters contemporary accounts of hard-pressed working-class women and men making their way through
substantial amounts of serious fiction and nonfiction. Alternatively, one encounters readers within the middle class
who fret over the potential of the penny tabloid to corrupt
all British citizens. For descriptions of working-class reading, see Davies, *Life as We Have Known It,* and Bell, *At the
Works.* For middle-class concerns, see testimony given to
the Royal Commission, for example vol. 1: 75; and vol. 2:
412, 460–461.

8 See Reeves, *Round About a Pound a Week* (21). Reeves's
analysis focused on working-class families living in London's Lambeth neighborhood.

9 *My Husband Still* was "compiled" by Helen Hamilton and introduced by John Galsworthy. As Galsworthy explains, the text was based on the journal of a working-class woman well known to Hamilton. After explaining the circumstances behind the writing, Galsworthy goes on to argue warmly against the likelihood of poorer working people resorting in any great numbers to divorce were it to be made more available. As it has turned out, the occupational classes most likely to divorce are precisely those at the lowest rung of the socio-economic ladder, the partly skilled, unskilled, members of the armed forces, and the unemployed (data are from a 1984 survey by Haskey, "Social Class and Socio-Economic Differentials in Divorce," reported in Burgoyne, *Divorce Matters,* 34).

10 Cockburn, *Best Seller,* 4. For further background on early twentieth-century popular novels, see Bennett's *How to Become an Author;* Hunter, *Edwardian Fiction,* chapter 5; E. V. Lucas, *Listener's Lure;* and Q. D. Leavis, *Fiction and the Reading Public.*

11 For Ford's comments, see the inaugural editorial, entitled "The Month," for the *English Review* (December 1908): 157–160, and his Foreword to *The English Review Book of Short Stories;* Wells, *An Experiment in Autobiography,* 416–417; and Forster, "Pessimism in Literature." For recent analyses of the dialogue between realism and feminism, see Ardis, *New Women, New Novels,* chapter 2, and Miller, *Rebel Women,* chapter 1.

12 The argument made by Ardis and Miller is bolstered by a contemporary late nineteenth-century account, Elizabeth Chapman's *Marriage Questions in Modern Fiction and Other Essays on Kindred Subjects* (1897). See also Chapman's views on divorce in the same collection ("The Decline of Divorce," 131–167, and "Why We Should Oppose Divorce," 195–223).

13 Rachel Blau DuPlessis's insightful *Writing Beyond the Ending* continues a superb series of critical works on narrative endings, beginning as early as Alan Friedman's *The Turn of the Novel* and enriched by Frank Kermode's *The Sense of*

an Ending. But there is a loss of insight, I believe, in focusing too intensely on how a novel closes. Novels with ultimately conventional endings often leave a legacy in the mind that disturbs, teases, provokes.

14 Miller finds that the Edwardian marriage novel assiduously avoids wifely adultery. I find the opposite in the novels that focus on divorce. Partly because they aim to resist the reigning legal tale on divorce—with its discrepant penalties for female and male adultery—many of these novels do explore wifely adultery, and often in sympathetic terms. See for example Anthony Hope, *Mrs. Maxon Protests*; Bennett, *Whom God Hath Joined*; Galsworthy, *The Country House*; Victoria Cross, *The Life Sentence*; Beatrice Harraden, *Interplay*; Vincent Brown, *Mayfield*; Braby, *The Honey of Romance*; Guy Thorne, *Divorce*; and C. A. Dawson Scott, *The Caddis Worm*. By contrast, the adulteries of the husbands in Diehl's *The Confessions of Perpetua*; Bennett's *Whom God Hath Joined*; M. E. Hughes's *Margot Munro*; F. E. Mills Young's *A Mistaken Marriage*; and *My Husband Still* are judged far more severely.

15 On the two suitor convention, see Miller, Jean Kennard, and H. M. Daleski.

16 As it is situated in Diehl's narrative, this dream reads as both a retrospective account of Perpetua's life with her husband, Colonel Delincourt, and an anticipation of the diphtheria she contracts from a visit to one of Delincourt's mistresses. The analogy between an abusive marriage and a fatal disease is important to the plot.

17 See Glendon, *Abortion and Divorce in Western Law*, Introduction and chapter 2. As America in the mid-1990s worriedly debates the current state of marriage and very meaning of "family values," this ambivalence toward divorce shows up as a constant theme. See for example Elizabeth Gleick's cover story for *Time*, "For Better, For Worse" (February 27, 1995): 48–56.

18 An interest in the contradictions that fuel narrative, literary and nonliterary, has become standard in current literary theory. In *Protocols of Reading*, Robert Scholes offers a cogent review and history of this interest and of the debate

it has engendered between deconstructionists and their opponents (chapter 2); Brooks's *Reading for the Plot* exemplifies a different approach as it contemplates narrative contradictions within a psychoanalytic description of the "erotics" of reading.

19 Nancy Armstrong's *Desire and Domestic Fiction* provides a fine analysis of the way English domestic novels between the eighteenth and nineteenth centuries reconfigured marriage—and middle-class identity itself—as private rather than public phenomena.

20 My proviso relates to a racist scene late in the novel when Ernestine, traveling alone in Egypt, is sexually approached by a "dark skinned" man. Generally open in her thinking and admiring of other cultures, Ernestine is revolted. With no discernable irony, the omniscient narrator explains it as the abhorrence of white for black, clean for dirty, superior race for inferior race.

21 The task of the King's Proctor was to discover any obstacles to the awarding of the *decree absolute.* In actuality a band of paid investigators, these detectives were active during the probationary six months following the *decree nisi,* seeking out information that would either incriminate the presumably innocent party or reveal collusion between the divorcing partners.

22 See DuPlessis's *Writing Beyond the Ending* for a useful description of the key elements of the romance plot (5).

23 Miller faults Bennett for not developing Phyllis. I see her as purposefully left alone. Equally interesting to me is Bennett's decision to imagine Lawrence constructing his identity through the quality of his marriage. Nor is he an isolated case: see also Sinclair's *The Combined Maze*; Cross's *The Life Sentence*; Braby's *The Honey of Romance*; Cleeve's *Woman and Moses*; Thorne's *Divorce*; Hobbes's *The Dream and the Business*; Gibbs's *The Custody of the Child*; Hunt's *The Doll*; Ward's *Daphne*; Wells's *The New Machiavelli*; James's *The Cage Unbarred*; Vane's *The Soul of a Man*; Smith's *Nevertheless*; and Dudeney's *The Third Floor.*

24 Published in 1909, Ward's novel takes on specific issues

being hotly debated in America during the decade, key among them the possibility of a national law on divorce. In 1905, President Roosevelt had requested Congress to compile data on American divorce laws and rates. In 1906, a National Congress, representing forty-two states and territories, met in Washington D.C., in hopes of drafting a uniform law. Ward herself was not in the States for this event, but did visit two years later, in 1908. She dined with the president and visited Mount Vernon and Niagara Falls. *Daphne* comes out of this visit. Never shy about her positions, she sent a copy to Arthur Conan Doyle, who wrote back, "Now please write the converse, and show how the too inelastic marriage laws of England bind a good woman to a sot, a maniac, and a criminal. That cause wants help badly" (in Enid Huws Jones, *Mrs. Humphrey Ward,* 152). See Phillips, *Putting Asunder,* for background on the American divorce reform movement and the obstacles it faced (468–470).

25 In the character of Leopold, Ward also complicates the role often given to the Jew in anti-divorce novels. A London lawyer, the Jew in many of the conservative novels is cast as a crafty figure of anti-Christian practices. In *Daphne,* both through Madeleine's memory of Leopold and through a Rembrandt painting owned by Daphne, the Jew is presented as a cruelly ostracized human being, his face stamped with melancholy and the premonition of disaster (55).

26 Ward actively opposed woman suffrage, among other feminist causes. See her novel, *Delia Blanchflower,* for a characteristic expression of her views.

27 See Hunter, *Edwardian Fiction,* for an analysis of the role the house plays in Edwardian fiction in general (chapter 13).

28 Writing of divorce in an American context, Edith Wharton plays out this complex concern for children. In *The Custom of the Country* (1913) she makes much of the devastating loneliness of young Paul. In *The Children* (1928), Judith, at fifteen, is forced to assume adult responsibility for a brood of neglected children.

29 Scholes, *Protocols of Reading,* 139, 141.
30 Hunt's language here is noteworthy in its contradictions. In late Victorian and Edwardian popular culture, the golliwog was an African-featured male doll. It originated in a series of stories for children by Florence and Bertha Upton (published between 1895 and 1910) and was duplicated as a soft doll as well as a wooden, varnished doll. A parallel in America would be the Black Sambo doll. Examples of the golliwog may be seen at the Toy Museum in Bethnal Green, London. Clearly Hunt introduces the image—and uses it again in the closing pages of the novel—as a positive figure. Little Timothy can love this doll. It replaces both the rags he has clung to and the princes and sailors he has rejected. And yet, Hunt's left hand takes away what her right hand gives to this dear, black doll. It was "ugly"; it was "black but comely, grotesque but clean" (290). For background on the golliwog and the Upton series, see *When Toys Come Alive* by Lois Rostow Kuznets.
31 Leotard, *Instructions paiennes,* 39.
32 See Carver's short story, "What We Talk About When We Talk About Love."
33 My language here is borrowed from Geertz's "Thick Description: Toward an Interpretive Theory of Culture."

Bibliography

Primary Sources

Fiction and Drama

Alexander, Mrs. [Annie French Hector]. *The Crumpled Leaf: A Vatican Mystery*. London: Henry J. Drane, 1911.

Annesley, Maude. *The Wine of Life*. London: John Lane, 1907.

Bennett, Arnold. *These Twain*. New York: George H. Doran, Co., 1915.

―――. *Whom God Hath Joined*. London: D. Nutt, 1906. Rept. Great Britain: Alan Sutton Publishing, Ltd., 1985.

Braby, Maud Churton. *The Honey of Romance: Being the Tragic Love Story of a Publisher's Wife*. London: T. W. Laurie, 1915.

Brown, Vincent. *Mayfield*. New York: Brentano's, 1912.

Chew, Doris Nield. *The Life and Writings of Ada Nield Chew*. London: Virago, 1982.

Cleeve, Lucas. *Woman and Moses*. London: Hurst and Blackett, 1902.

Cotterell, Constance. *The Honest Trespass*. London: Eveleigh Nash, Co., 1911.

Croker, Bithia Mary. *The Serpent's Tooth*. London: Hutchinson and Co., 1912.

Cross, Victoria [Vivian Cory]. *The Life Sentence*. London: John Long, Ltd., 1912.

Diehl, Alice M. *The Confessions of Perpetua*. London: Stanley Paul and Co., 1912.

Dudeney, Mrs. Henry. *The Third Floor*. London: Methuen, 1901.

Galsworthy, John. *The Country House*. New York: G.P. Putnam and Sons, 1907. Rept. New York: Charles Scribner's Sons, 1920.

―――. *In Chancery*. London: Heinemann, 1920.

BIBLIOGRAPHY

Gibbs, Philip. *The Custody of the Child*. London: Hutchinson and Co., 1914.

Gibson, Lettice Susan. *The Oakum Pickers*. London: Methuen and Co., Ltd., 1912.

Hamilton, Cicely and Christopher St. John. "How the Vote Was Won." 1909. Chicago: The Dramatic Publishing Co., 1910.

Hamilton, Helen, ed. *My Husband Still: A Working Woman's Story*. Foreword by John Galsworthy. London: G. Bell and Sons, 1914.

Hamilton, M. [Mary Churchill Luck]. *The First Claim*. London: Methuen and Co., 1906.

Harraden, Beatrice. *Interplay*. London: Methuen and Co., 1908.

Herbert, A. P. *Holy Deadlock*. Harmondsworth, Eng.: Penguin Books, 1934.

Hine, Muriel [Mrs. Sidney Coxon]. *April Panhasard*. London: John Lane, 1913.

Hobbes, John Oliver [Pearl Craigie]. *The Dream and the Business*. London: T. F. Unwin, 1906.

Hope, Anthony [Anthony Hope Hawkins]. *Mrs. Maxon Protests*. London: Methuen and Co., Ltd., 1911.

Howell, Constance. *Mrs. Charteris*. London: John Ouseley Ltd., 1911.

Hughes, M. E. *Margot Munro*. London: Mills and Boon, 1910.

Hunt, Violet. *The Doll: A Happy Story*. London: Stanley Paul and Co., 1911.

James, Gertie De S. Wentworth. *The Cage Unbarred: Being the Story of a Woman Who Was Dull*. London: Everett and Co., Ltd., 1913.

James, Henry. *What Maisie Knew*. London: Heinemann, 1897.

Maxwell, William Babington. *Remedy Against Sin*. London: Hutchinson and Co., 1920.

————. *The Rest Cure*. London: Methuen and Co., Ltd., 1910.

Nevinson, Margaret. *The Spoilt Child of the Law*. London: Women's Freedom League, 1913.

Phibbs, L. S. "Jim's Leg." *Votes for Women* (January 29, 1911). Rept. Julie Holledge. *Innocent Flowers: Women in the Edwardian Theatre*. London: Virago Press, 1981.

Roberts, Morley. *Hearts of Women*. London: Eveleigh Nash Co., 1919.

Russell, Countess. *An Excellent Mystery*. London: Stephen Swift and Co., Ltd., 1912.

Scott, C. A. Dawson [Catharine Amy Dawson Scott]. *The Caddis Worm: or Episodes in the Life of Richard and Catharine Blake*. London: Hurst and Blackett, Ltd., 1914.

Shaw, George Bernard. *Getting Married*. New York: Brentano's, 1913.

Sinclair, May. *The Combined Maze*. London: Hutchinson and Co., 1913.

Smith, Isabel. *Nevertheless*. London: Alston Rivers Ltd., 1913.

Syrett, Netta. *Drender's Daughter*. London: Chatto and Windus, 1911.

Thorne, Guy [Cyril Arthur Gull]. *Divorce*. London: Greening and Co., Ltd., 1911.

Troubridge, Lady. *The First Law*. London: Mills and Boon. 1909.

Vane, Derek. *The Soul of a Man*. London: Holden and Hardingham, 1913.

Ward, Mary Augusta. *Daphne; or, Marriage a La Mode*. London: Cassell and Co., Ltd., 1909.

———. *Delia Blanchflower*. New York: Hearst's International Library, 1914.

Waugh, Alec. *Nor Many Waters*. London: Chapman and Hall, Ltd., 1928.

Wells, H. G. *The New Machiavelli*. London: Cassell and Co., Ltd., 1910.

Wharton, Edith. *The Children*. New York: D. Appleton and Co., 1928.

———. *The Custom of the Country*. 1913. Rept. New York: Charles Scribner's Sons, 1941.

Young, F. E. Mills [Florence Ethel Mills Young]. *A Mistaken Marriage*. London: John Lane, 1908.

BIBLIOGRAPHY

Nonfiction

Annual Digest of the Times Law Reports. London: George Edward Wright.

Balfour, Lady Frances. *Ne Obliviscaris: Dinna Forget.* London: Hodder and Stoughton, 1930.

Barnes, Henry Gorell. "Divorce Law and Its Reform." *The Contemporary Review* 103 (1913): 62–69.

Bell, Florence. *At the Works: A Study of a Manufacturing Town.* 1907. Rept. London: Virago Press, 1985.

Bennett, Arnold. *How to Become an Author: A Practical Guide.* London: The Literary Correspondence College, 1903; 1914.

Black, Clementina, ed. *Married Women's Work: Being the Report of an Enquiry Undertaken by the Women's Industrial Council, Incorporated.* London: G. Bell and Sons Ltd., 1915.

Braby, Maud Churton. *Modern Marriage and How to Bear It.* London: T. Werner Laurie, 1909.

Bremner, Christina Sinclair. *Divorce and Morality.* London: Frank Palmer, 1912.

Chapman, Cecil. *Marriage and Divorce: Some Needed Reforms in Church and State.* London: David Nutt, 1911.

———. *The Poor Man's Court of Justice: Twenty-Five Years as a Metropolitan Magistrate.* London: Hodder and Stoughton Ltd., 1925.

Chapman, Elizabeth Rachel. *Marriage Questions in Modern Fiction, and Other Essays on Kindred Subjects.* New York: The Bodley Head, 1897.

Crackanthorpe, Montague. "Marriage, Divorce, and Eugenics." *The Nineteenth Century* 68 (1910): 686–702.

Davies, Margaret Llewelyn. *Working Women and Divorce: An Account of Evidence Given on Behalf of the Women's Co-operative Guild before the Royal Commission on Divorce.* London: David Nutt, 1911.

———, ed. *Life as We Have Known It: By Co-operative Working Women* (London: Hogarth Press, 1931; rpt. New York: W. W. Norton, 1975).

Day, Father Henry, S.J. *Marriage, Divorce, and Morality.* London: Burns and Oates, Ltd., 1912.

BIBLIOGRAPHY

"Divorce Report." *The Saturday Review* (November 16, 1912): 602–603.

Doyle, Arthur Conan. Preface. *Divorce and Morality* by Christina Sinclair Bremner. London: Frank Palmer, 1912.

"Falling Birth Rate: Registrar General's Alarming Figures." *Evening Standard and St. James Gazette* (January 30, 1909): 1.

Ford, Ford Madox. "The Month." *English Review* 1 (December, 1908): 157–160.

———. Foreword. *The English Review Book of Short Stories*, compiled by Horace Shipp. London: Samson Low, Marston, and Co., 1932.

Forster, E. M. "Pessimism in Literature." 1907. Rept. *Albergo Empedocle and Other Writings*. George H. Thomson, ed. New York: Liveright, 1971: 129–145.

Gates, Richard T. *Divorce or Separation: Which?,* with an introductory note by C. W. Saleeby, F.R. S.E. London: Divorce Law Reform Union, 1910.

Gibbs, Philip. *The Eighth Year: A Vital Problem of Married Life*. London: Williams and Norgate, 1913.

Hamilton, Cicely. *Marriage as a Trade*. New York: Moffat, Yard, and Co., 1909.

Haynes, E.S.P. *Divorce as It Might Be*. Cambridge, Eng.: W. Heffer and Sons, Ltd., 1915.

———. *Divorce Problems of Today*. Cambridge, Eng.: W. Heffer and Sons, Ltd., 1912.

Holmes, Thomas. "The New Licensing Bill." *The Contemporary Review* 81 (1902): 508–515.

Jenks, Edward. *Husband and Wife in the Law*. London: J. M. Dent and Co., 1909.

Kitchin, S. B. *A History of Divorce*. London: Chapman and Hall, Ltd., 1912.

Lucas, E. V. *Listener's Lure: An Oblique Narration*. London: Methuen and Co., Ltd., 1906.

Marsden, Dora. "Woman: Endowed or Free?" *The Freewoman: A Weekly Feminist Review* 1 (February 29, 1912): 281–283.

———. "Women Endowed." *The Freewoman: A Weekly Feminist Review* 1 (March 14, 1912): 321–323.

Masterman, C. F. G. *The Condition of England*. London: Methuen and Co., 1909.

BIBLIOGRAPHY

Plowden, Alfred Chichele. *Grain or Chaff?: The Autobiography of a Police Magistrate.* London: Thomas Nelson and Sons, 1914.

Question of English Divorce: An Essay. anon. London: Grant Richards, 1903.

Reeves, Magdalen Stuart Pember. *Round About a Pound a Week.* London: G. Bell and Sons, Ltd., 1913.

Report of the Royal Commission on Divorce and Matrimonial Causes: Minutes of Evidence, 1912–1913. Vols. 1–4. cmnd. 6478. London: His Majesty's Stationery Office, 1912.

Russell, Earl. *Divorce.* London: Heinemann, 1912.

Saleeby, C. W. Introduction. *Divorce or Separation: Which?,* by Richard T. Gates. London: Divorce Law Reform Union, 1910.

Schreiner, Olive. *Woman and Labour.* London: T. F. Unwin, 1911.

Seventieth Annual Report of the Registrar General of Births, Deaths, and Marriages in England and Wales for 1907. London: His Majesty's Stationery Office, 1909.

Shaw, George Bernard. Preface. *Getting Married.* New York: Brentano's, 1913.

Stone, Darwell, D.D. *Divorce and Remarriage: An Address on the Majority and Minority Reports of the Royal Commission on Divorce and Matrimonial Causes.* London: Longmans, Green, and Co., 1913.

Swanwick, Helena Maria Lucy. *The Future of the Women's Movement.* London: G. Bell and Sons, 1913.

———. *I Have Been Young.* London: Victor Gollancz Ltd., 1935.

Tibbets, Charles. *Marriage Making and Marriage Breaking,* with an introduction by A. C. Plowden. London: Stanley Paul and Co., 1911.

Wells, H. G. *An Experiment in Autobiography: Discoveries and Conclusions of an Ordinary Brain.* New York: The Macmillan Co., 1934.

———. "Mr. Wells to the Attack: Freewomen and Endowment." *The Freewoman: A Weekly Feminist Review* 1 (March 7, 1912): 301–302.

————. "Woman Endowed." *The Freewoman: A Feminist Weekly Review* 1 (March 21, 1912): 341–342.

West, Rebecca. "The Divorce Commission: A Report That Will Not Become Law." *The Clarion,* 29 November 1912. Rpt. in *The Young Rebecca: Writings of Rebecca West 1911–1917,* ed. Jane Marcus. Bloomington: Indiana University Press, 1982:124–127.

Secondary Sources

Adams, Carol. *Ordinary Lives a Hundred Years Ago.* London: Virago Press, 1982.

Altick, Richard D. *Deadly Encounters: Two Victorian Sensations.* Philadelphia: University of Pennsylvania Press, 1986.

————. *Writers, Readers, and Occasions.* Columbus: Ohio State University Press, 1989.

Ardis, Ann L. "Ada Nield Chew." *Dictionary of Literary Biography: British Short Fiction Writers* 135. Detroit: Gale Research, Inc., 1994: 47–52.

————. *New Women, New Novels: Feminism and Early Modernism.* New Brunswick, N.J.: Rutgers University Press, 1990.

Armstrong, Nancy. *Desire and Domestic Fiction: A Political History of the Novel.* New York: Oxford University Press, 1987.

Baker, Ernest A. *A Guide to the Best Fiction in English:* 1913. New York: Macmillan, 1913.

Batchelor, John. *The Edwardian Novelists.* New York: St. Martin's Press, 1982.

Bauer, Dale. *Feminist Dialogics: A Theory of Failed Community.* Albany: State University of New York Press, 1988.

Bennett, W. Lance, and Martha S. Feldman. *Reconstructing Reality in the Courtroom: Justice and Judgment in American Culture.* New Brunswick, N.J.: Rutgers University Press, 1981.

Berenson, Edward. *The Trial of Madame Caillaux*. Berkeley and Los Angeles: University of California Press, 1992.

Bottomley, Anne. "What Is Happening to Family Law: A Feminist Critique of Conciliation." *Women-in-Law: Explorations in Law, Family, and Sexuality*, ed. Julia Brophy and Carol Smart. London: Routledge and Kegan Paul, Ltd., 1985: 162–185.

Brake, Laurel. "The Old Journalism and the New: Forms of Cultural Production in London in the 1880s." *Papers for the Millions: The New Journalism in Britain, 1850 to 1914*, ed. Joel H. Wiener. New York: Greenwood Press, 1988: 1–24.

Brooks, Peter. *Reading for the Plot: Design and Intention in Narrative*. New York: Alfred A. Knopf, 1984.

Brophy, Julia. "Custody Law, Child Care, and Inequality in Britain." *Child Custody and the Politics of Gender*, ed. Carol Smart and Selma Sevenhuijsen. London: Routledge, 1989: 217– 242.

——— and Carol Smart. "Locating Law: A Discussion of the Place of Law in Feminist Politics." *Women-in-Law: Explorations in Law, Family, and Sexuality*, ed. Julia Brophy and Carol Smart. London: Routledge and Kegan Paul, Ltd., 1985: 1–20.

——— and Carol Smart, eds. *Women-in-Law: Explorations in Law, Family, and Sexuality*. London: Routledge and Kegan Paul, Ltd., 1985.

Brown, Joan C. *In Search of a Policy: The Rationale for Social Security Provision for One Parent Families*. London: Roger Booth Associates; National Council for One Parent Families, nd.

Buckley, Suzann. "The Family and the Role of Women." *The Edwardian Age: Conflict and Stability 1900–1914*. Alan O'Day, ed. Hamden, Conn.: Archon Books, 1979: 133–143.

Burgoyne, Jacqueline, Roger Ormrod, and Martin Richards. *Divorce Matters*. Harmondsworth, Eng.: Penguin Books, 1987.

Carver, Raymond. *What We Talk About When We Talk About Love*. New York: Alfred A. Knopf, 1981.

Clark, David, and Douglas Haldane. *Wedlocked? Intervention*

and Research in Marriage. Cambridge: Polity Press and Basil
Blackwell, 1990.

Clulow, Christopher, and Christopher Vincent. *In the Child's
Best Interests? Divorce Court Welfare and the Search for a Settlement.* New York: Sweet and Maxwell, 1987.

Cockburn, Claud. *Best Seller: The Books That Everyone Read
1900–1939.* London: Sidgwick and Jackson, 1972.

Cover, Robert M. "Nomos and Narrative." *Harvard Law Review* 97 (1983): 4–68.

Craik, Jennifer. *The Face of Fashion: Cultural Studies in Fashion.* London: Routledge, 1994.

Cross, Colin. *The Liberals in Power* 1905–1914. London: Bar-
rie and Rockliff, with Pall Mall Press, 1963.

Daims, Diva, and Janet Grimes, eds. *Toward a Feminist Tradition: An Annotated Bibliography of Novels in English by
Women 1891–1920.* New York: Garland, 1981.

Daleski, H. M. *The Divided Heroine: A Recurrent Pattern in Six
English Novels.* New York: Holmes and Meier, 1984.

Danziger, Danny. *Lost Hearts: Talking About Divorce.* London: Bloomsbury Press, 1992.

Davis, Gwynn, and Mervyn Murch. *Grounds for Divorce.* Oxford, Eng.: Clarendon Press, 1988.

Deegan, Thomas. "No-Fault Divorce Films: Hollywood's
Changing Morality." *Cineaste: America's Leading Magazine
on the Art and Politics of the Cinema* 15 (1986): 24–27.

Delgado, Richard. "Storytelling for Oppositionists and Others: A Plea for Narrative." *Michigan Law Review* 87 (1989):
2411–2441.

DeMontmorency, J.E.G. *John Gorell Barnes: First Lord Gorell:
A Memoir,* with an introduction by Ronald, Third Lord
Gorell. London: John Murray, 1920.

DuPlessis, Rachel Blau. *Writing Beyond the Ending: Narrative
Strategies of Twentieth-Century Women Writers.* Bloomington: Indiana University Press, 1985.

Dworkin, Ronald. "Law as Interpretation." *Critical Inquiry* 9
(1982): 179–200.

Dyhouse, Carol. *Feminism and the Family in England 1880–
1939.* Oxford: Basil Blackwell, 1989.

———. "Good Wives and Little Mothers: Social Anxieties

and the Schoolgirl's Curriculum, 1890–1920." *Oxford Review of Education* 3 (1977): 21–35.

Eekelaar, John, and Mavis Maclean. *Maintenance After Divorce*. Oxford, Eng.: Clarendon Press, 1986.

———. *Regulating Divorce*. Oxford, Eng.: Clarendon Press, 1991.

Fish, Stanley. "Working on the Chain Gang: Interpretation in the Law and in Literary Criticism." *Critical Inquiry* 9 (1982): 201–216.

Folbre, Nancy. "The Unproductive Housewife: Her Evolution in Nineteenth Century Economic Thought." *Signs* 16 (1991): 463–484.

Friedman, Alan. *The Turn of the Novel*. New York: Oxford University Press, 1967.

Geertz, Clifford. "Local Knowledge: Fact and Law in Comparative Perspective." *Local Knowledge: Further Essays in Interpretive Anthropology*. New York: Basic Books, 1983: 167–234.

———. "Thick Description: Toward an Interpretive Theory of Culture." *The Interpretation of Cultures*. New York: Basic Books, 1973: 3–30.

Gernsheim, Alison. *Victorian and Edwardian Fashion: A Photographic Survey*. New York: Dover Publications, 1981. Published in England as *Fashion and Reality: 1840–1914*. London: Faber and Faber, 1963.

Gilbert, Bentley B. *The Evolution of National Insurance in Great Britain*. London: Michael Joseph, 1966.

Gittins, Diana. *Fair Sex: Family Size and Structure in Britain, 1900–1939*. New York: St. Martin's Press, 1982.

Gleick, Elizabeth. "For Better, For Worse: Should This Marriage Be Saved?" *Time* 145 (February 27, 1995): 48–56.

Glendon, Mary Ann. *Abortion and Divorce in Western Law: American Failures, European Challenges*. Cambridge, Mass.: Harvard University Press, 1987.

Goody, Jack. *The Development of the Family and Marrige in Europe*. Cambridge, Eng.: Cambridge University Press, 1983.

Hammerton, A. James. *Cruelty and Companionship: Conflict in Nineteenth-Century Married Life*. London: Routledge, 1992.

Harris, Janice H. "Challenging the Script of the Heterosexual Couple: Three Marriage Novels by May Sinclair. *Papers on Language and Literature* 29 (1993): 436–458.

———. "Feminist Representations of Wives and Work: An 'Almost Irreconcilable' Edwardian Debate." *Women's Studies* 22 (1993): 309–333.

———. "Wifely Silence and Speech in Three Marriage Novels by H. G. Wells. *Studies in the Novel* 26 (Winter, 1994): 404–419.

Hartman, K. Donald. *Themes and Settings in Fiction: A Bibliography of Bibliographies*. New York: Greenwood Press, 1988.

Haskey, John. "The Proportion of Marriages Ending in Divorce." *Population Trends* 27 (1982): 4–8.

Holcombe, Lee. *Wives and Property: Reform of the Married Women's Property Law in Nineteenth-Century England*. Toronto and Buffalo: University of Toronto Press, 1983.

Holledge, Julie. *Innocent Flowers: Women in the Edwardian Theatre*. London: Virago Press, 1981.

Hunter, Jefferson. *Edwardian Fiction*. Cambridge, Mass.: Harvard University Press, 1982.

Hynes, Samuel. *The Edwardian Turn of Mind*. Princeton: Princeton University Press, 1968.

Jones, Enid Huws. *Mrs. Humphrey Ward*. London: Heinemann, 1973.

Kennard, Jean E. *Victims of Convention*. Hamden, Conn.: Archon, 1978.

Kermode, Frank. *The Sense of an Ending: Studies in the Theory of Fiction*. New York: Oxford University Press, 1967.

Kiernan, K., and M. Wicks. *Family Change and Future Policy*. London: Family Policy Studies Center, 1990.

Kirp, David L., Mark G. Yudof, and Marlene Strong Franks. *Gender Justice*. Chicago: University of Chicago Press, 1986.

Kreiswirth, Martin. "Trusting the Tale: The Narrativist Turn in the Human Sciences." *New Literary History* 23 (1992): 629–657.

Kuznets, Lois Rostow. *When Toys Come Alive: Narratives of Animation, Metamorphosis, and Development*. New Haven, Conn.: Yale University Press, 1994.

BIBLIOGRAPHY

Larkin, Philip. "MCMXIV." *The Whitsun Weddings: Poems by Philip Larkin*. London: Faber and Faber, 1964.

Lauterbach, Edward S., and Eugene Davis. *The Transitional Age: British Literature 1880–1920*. Troy, N.Y.: Whitson Publishing Co., Inc., 1973.

Leavis, Q. D. *Fiction and the Reading Public*. London: Chatto and Windus, 1932.

Lee, Alan J. *The Origins of the Popular Press in England: 1855–1914*. London: Croom Helm, 1976.

Lewis, Jane. *The Politics of Motherhood: Child and Maternal Welfare in England, 1900–1939*. London: Croom Helm, 1980.

———. *Women in England 1870–1950: Sexual Divisions and Social Change*. Bloomington: Indiana University Press, 1984.

Leotard, Jean-François. *Instructions Paiennes*. Paris: Galilee, 1977.

Lopez, Gerald. "Lay Lawyering." *UCLA Law Review* 32 (1984): 1–60.

Lovell, Colin Rhys. *English Constitutional and Legal History: A Survey*. New York: Oxford University Press, 1962.

MacKinnon, Catharine A. "Feminism, Marxism, Method, and the State: Toward Feminist Jurisprudence: A Viewpoint." *Signs* 8 (1983): 635–658.

McGregor, O. R. *Divorce in England: A Centenary Study*. London: Heinemann, 1957.

Markham, Violet. *May Tennant: A Portrait*. London: The Falcon Press, 1949.

Massaro, Toni. "Empathy, Legal Storytelling, and the Rule of Law: Old Words, Old Wounds." *Michigan Law Review* 87 (1989): 2099–2127.

Miller, Jane Eldridge. *Rebel Women: Feminism, Modernism, and the Edwardian Novel*. London: Virago Press, 1994.

Minney, R. J. *The Edwardian Age*. Boston: Little, Brown and Co., 1964.

Mitchell, W.J.T. "Representation." *Critical Terms for Literary Study*. Frank Lentricchia and Thomas McLaughlin, eds. Chicago: University of Chicago Press, 1990: 11–22.

Mullan, Bob. *Perfect Partners? Love, Sex, Marriage, and Friendship*. Great Britain: Boxtree, Ltd., 1988.

BIBLIOGRAPHY

O'Day, Alan, ed. *The Edwardian Age: Conflict and Stability 1900–1914*. Hamden, Conn.: Archon Books, 1979.

Phillips, Roderick. *Putting Asunder: A History of Divorce in Western Society*. Cambridge, Eng.: Cambridge University Press, 1988.

Pike, Edgar Royston. *Human Documents of the Lloyd George Era*. New York: St. Martin's Press, 1972.

Priestley, J. B. *The Edwardians*. New York: Harper and Row Publishers, 1970.

Read, Donald. *Edwardian England*. New Brunswick, N.J.: Rutgers University Press, 1982.

Read, Piers Paul. "To Part at Last Without a Kiss." *The Spectator,* January 16, 1993: 31.

Reissman, Catherine Kohler. *Divorce Talk: Women and Men Make Sense of Personal Relationships*. New Brunswick, N.J.: Rutgers University Press, 1990.

Rhode, Deborah L. *Justice and Gender: Sex Discrimination and the Law*. Cambridge, Mass.: Harvard University Press, 1989.

Roe, Emery. "Applied Narrative Analysis: The Tangency of Literary Criticism, Social Science, and Policy Analysis." *New Literary History* 23 (1992): 555–581.

Rogal, Samuel J. *A Chronological Outline of British Literature*. Westport, Conn.: Greenwood Press, 1980.

Rolley, Katrina, and Caroline Aish. *Fashion in Photographs, 1900–1920*. London: B. T. Batsford, Ltd., 1992.

Rose, Phyllis. *Parallel Lives: Five Victorian Marriages*. New York: Random House, 1983.

Ross, Ellen. "'Fierce Questions and Taunts': Married Life in Working-Class London, 1870– 1914," *Feminist Studies* 8 (Fall 1982): 575–602.

Royal Courts of Justice: An Illustrated Guide. 3rd ed. Prepared by the High Court Journalists' Association. London: Cadra House, Ltd., 1977.

Royal Courts of Justice: An Introduction for Visitors. January 1990. Available at the Superintendent's Office, Royal Courts of Justice, London.

Russell, Douglas. *Costume History and Style*. Englewood Cliffs, N.J.: Prentice-Hall, Inc., 1983.

Savage, Gail. "Divorce and the Law in England and France Prior to the First World War." *Journal of Social History* 21 (1988): 499–513.

Scales, Ann C. "The Emergence of Feminist Jurisprudence: An Essay." *Yale Law Journal* 95 (1986): 1373–1403.

Schepple, Kim Lane. "Facing Facts in Legal Interpretation." *Representations* 30 (1990): 42–77.

———. "Foreword: Telling Stories." *Michigan Law Review* 87 (1989): 2073–2098.

Schneider, Elizabeth, Mary Dunlap, Michael Lavery, and John DeWitt Gregory. "Workshop: Lesbians, Gays, and Feminists at the Bar—Translating Personal Experience into Effective Legal Argument." *Women's Rights Law Reporter* 10 (1988): 107–141.

Scholes, Robert. *Protocols of Reading*. New Haven, Conn.: Yale University Press, 1989.

Shackleton, Fiona, and Olivia Timbs. *The Divorce Handbook: A Step-by-Step Guide to the Divorce Process*. London: Harper Collins, 1992.

Shanley, Mary Lyndon. *Feminism, Marriage, and the Law in Victorian England:1850–1895*. Princeton, N.J.: Princeton University Press, 1989.

Smart, Carol. *The Ties that Bind: Law, Marriage, and the Reproduction of Patriarchal Relations*. London: Routledge, 1984.

———. "Locating Law: A Discussion of the Place of Law in Feminist Politics." *Women-in-Law: Explorations in Law, Family, and Sexuality*, ed. Julia Brophy and Carol Smart. London: Routledge and Kegan Paul, 1985: 1–20.

——— and Julia Brophy, eds. *Women-in-Law: Explorations in Law, Family, and Sexuality*. London: Routledge and Kegan Paul, 1985.

——— and Selma Sevenhuijsen, eds. *Child Custody and the Politics of Gender*. London: Routledge, 1989.

Stone, Lawrence. *Road to Divorce: England 1530–1987*. New York: Oxford University Press, 1990.

Strachey, Ray. *Millicent Garrett Fawcett*. London: J. Murray, 1931.

BIBLIOGRAPHY

Thompson, Paul. *The Edwardians: The Remaking of British Society*. Bloomington: Indiana University Press, 1975.

Tilly, Louise, and Joan W. Scott. *Women, Work, and Family*. New York: Holt, Rinehart, and Winston, 1978.

Weitzman, Lenore J. *The Divorce Revolution: The Unexpected Social and Economic Consequences for Women and Children in America*. New York: Free Press, 1985.

White, James Boyd. *Heracles' Bow: Essays on the Rhetoric and Poetics of the Law*. Madison: University of Wisconsin Press, 1985.

Wiener, Joel H., ed. *Papers for the Millions: The New Journalism in Britain, 1850s to 1914*. Westport, Conn.: Greenwood Press, 1988.

A B O U T   T H E   A U T H O R

Janice Hubbard Harris is a professor of English and Women's Studies at the University of Wyoming.